JUDITH A. CORBELLI

THE ART OF DEATH IN GRAECO-ROMAN EGYPT

SHIRE EGYPTOLOGY

Cover illustrations
(Left) Mummy case of Taminis from Akhmim.
(Top right) Clay-ground class cinerary urn from Alexandria.
(Bottom right) Detail of Hellenistic stela from Alexandria. (After Breccia)

For my sons, David and Edward Corbelli,
in memory of my late parents,
James and Susannah Turnbull.

British Library Cataloguing in Publication Data:
Corbelli, Judith A.
The art of death in Graeco-Roman Egypt. – (Shire Egyptology)
1. Sepulchral monuments – Egypt
2. Funeral rites and ceremonies – Egypt
3. Art, Classical – Egypt
4. Egypt – Civilization – 332 B.C. – 638 A.D. – Greek influences
I. Title 709.3'2
ISBN-10: 0 7478 0647 0.

Published in 2006 by
SHIRE PUBLICATIONS LTD
Cromwell House, Church Street, Princes Risborough,
Buckinghamshire HP27 9AA, UK.

Series Editor: Angela P. Thomas

ISBN-10: 0 7478 0647 0; ISBN-13: 978 0 7478 0647 9.

Number 28 in the Shire Egyptology series.

First published 2006.

Printed in Malta by Gutenberg Press Ltd, Gudja Road, Tarxien PLA19, Malta.

Contents

List of illustrations

Chronology

(Based on W. J. Murnane, *The Penguin Guide to Ancient Egypt*, 1983.)

Predynastic	before 3050 BC	
Early Dynastic	3050 to 2686 BC	Dynasties I to II
Old Kingdom	2686 to 2181 BC	Dynasties III to VI
First Intermediate Period	2181 to 2040 BC	Dynasties VII to XI (1)
Middle Kingdom	2040 to 1782 BC	Dynasties XI (2) to XII
Second Intermediate Period	1782 to 1570 BC	Dynasties XIII to XVII
New Kingdom	1570 to 1070 BC	Dynasties XVIII to XX
Third Intermediate Period	1070 to 664 BC	Dynasties XXI to XXV
Late Period	664 to 332 BC	Dynasties XXVI to XXXI

GRAECO-ROMAN PERIOD

Macedonian Kings 332 to 305 BC
323 *Ptolemy I, governor after death of Alexander the Great*

Ptolemaic Period 305 to 30 BC
305–282 *Ptolemy I Soter*
285–246 *Ptolemy II Philadelphus*
246–222 *Ptolemy III Euergetes*
222–204 *Ptolemy IV Philopator*
204–181 *Ptolemy V Epiphanes*
181–145 *Ptolemy VI Philometer*
145 *Ptolemy VII Eupator*
145–116 *Ptolemy VIII Euergetes II Physcon*
116–107 *Ptolemy IX Soter II Lathyros*
107–88 *Ptolemy X Alexandros*
88–80 *Restoration of Ptolemy IX*
80 *Ptolemy XI Alexandros II*
80–58 *Ptolemy XII Neos Dionysos Auletes*
58–55 *Berenike*
55–51 *Restoration of Ptolemy XII*
51–47 *Ptolemy XIII*
51–30 *Cleopatra VII Thea Philopator*
47–44 *Ptolemy XIV*
44–30 *Ptolemy XV Caesarion*

Roman Period 30 BC to AD 395
30 BC–AD 14 *Augustus*
14–68 Julio-Claudian Dynasty
69–96 Flavian Dynasty
96–98 *Nerva*
98–117 *Trajan*
117–138 *Hadrian*
138–192 Antonine Dynasty
192–235 Severan Dynasty
235–284 Over thirty minor rulers
284–324 *Diocletian* and Tetrarchs
306–363 Constantinian Dynasty
364–392 Valentinian Dynasty
379–450 Theodosian Dynasty

1
Historical background

In 332 BC Alexander the Great annexed Egypt to his expanding empire and, in 331 BC, founded a new capital city – Alexandria. On his death in 323 BC Egypt was apportioned to his general, Ptolemy, whose dynasty reigned until the death of Cleopatra VII in 30 BC. Under the Ptolemies' leadership, military men, merchants, artisans, entrepreneurs and academics from all over the Hellenistic world flocked to Egypt to seek their fortune in the land of the Nile. To cater for the mass of immigrants, land was reclaimed, settlements expanded, and new ones founded. All important posts were given to 'Hellenes' and the only way to get on was to adopt a Greek name and learn the official language – Greek. This encouraged ambitious Egyptians to become bilingual and, as time passed, there was a further mixing, through marriage, of an already ethnically diverse population. Administration was largely controlled through the temple foundations of the old order and religion played a big part in maintaining stability. The Greek settlers assimilated their own gods with the age-old Egyptian ones, and now, to meet the needs of everyone, a new god was introduced – Serapis – an amalgam of the Egyptian gods Osiris and Apis and the Greek gods Zeus, Helios and Dionysus – a wise political move to reduce friction.

Roman rule came to Egypt with Octavian's conquest of Cleopatra in 30 BC and there was again an increase in immigration and an expansion of settlements and large estates. These settlements have yielded a wealth of papyri, which have provided us with more comprehensive information on the public and private life of all classes of society than we have for any other period in Egypt's long history.

From the point of view of the archaeology of death, too, the material reflects the ethnic diversity of the population. However, few Graeco-Roman cemeteries have been fully excavated, the focus of interest over the centuries being on Pharaonic Egypt, and much of the funerary material remains unprovenanced or misclassified. The recovery of painted mummy portraits in the Fayum at the end of the nineteenth century focused attention on the funerary remains of the period, but the real increase in interest came in the later twentieth century, when spectacular discoveries were made in the necropoleis of Alexandria and the north coast towns and the cemeteries of the oases. The vast archaeological evidence indicates a wide variety of burial procedures, and the purpose of this book is to bring some of the material together in order to give an overview of funerary practices observed by the ethnically diverse population of Graeco-Roman Egypt.

Funerary rites

After death, in the Greek and Roman world, the body was washed and dressed in a shroud and a coin was placed in the mouth or hand to pay for the journey to the underworld. There then followed the *prothesis*, the body being laid out for a prescribed period to provide time for mourning and sacrifice, and finally the *ekphora* or funerary procession and deposition in the tomb. Pliny and Plutarch relate that portrait masks and busts of the deceased were carried in the Roman funeral procession and subsequently kept in cupboards at home. Rituals including sacrifices, libations, banquets, singing and dancing were performed at the tomb on the day of the funeral and on other anniversaries and festivals of the dead. Burial guilds existed in the Roman world whereby members paid contributions in advance for their funerals. Funerary procedures in Egypt would have been modified to incorporate mummification, a longer period of time being required for the desiccation and preservation of the body, and contemporary papyri refer to the process of mummification being carried out by 'slitters', 'curers' and 'preparers of mummies'. A period of approximately forty days seems to have been the interval between death and the wrapping of the corpse, and the poorly preserved and maggot-ridden condition of some mummies indicates a decline in the standard of mummification. Cicero, Diodorus and Strabo relate that, in contrast to Egyptian tradition, mummies of the period were kept above ground for a period of time, which may account for the damaged nature of many examples.

2
Rock-cut tombs

A wide variety of tomb types occurs, ranging from simple pit graves to rock-cut chamber tombs and hypogea, and many earlier tombs were re-used. Above-ground structures, where they exist, range from simple markers to larger multi-chambered structures, and types vary from place to place. Decoration, too, varies widely.

Alexandria

Strabo describes Alexandria's burial ground as 'Necropolis' – 'city of the dead', a place of tombs, gardens and embalmers' workshops. Excavations in the city have revealed several cemeteries with pit graves and rock-cut chamber tombs, of various types, and multi-chambered *hypogea* are a particular feature. Two basic types exist: *peristyle*, with chambers arranged around a central pillared court; and *oikos*, with chambers in linear formation (figure 1); both are accessed by rock-cut staircases. Essentially family tombs, the hypogea are subsequently enlarged with additional chambers, niches and loculi to accommodate

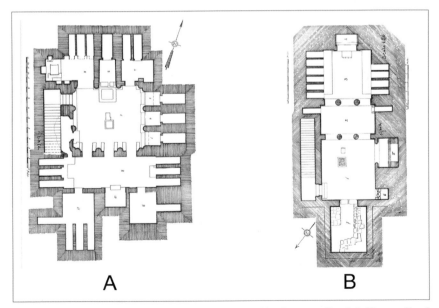

A   B

1. Alexandrian hypogea: (a) peristyle type, Tomb 1; (b) *oikos* type, Tomb 2, Necropolis of Mustapha Kamel, Alexandria (mid third to early second century BC). (After Adriani)

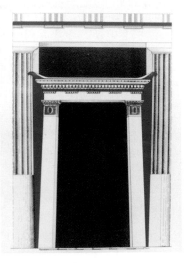

2. (Above) Portico of peristyle court, Tomb 1, Necropolis of Mustapha Kamel, Alexandria (mid third to early second century BC). (Right) Reconstruction drawing of painted portal. (After Adriani. Graphics courtesy of Derek Edwards)

further interments. Their form and decoration throw valuable light on the style of contemporary domestic and public buildings.

In the Ptolemaic Period, decoration consists of rock-cut features based on the Greek orders of architecture, such as the Doric peristyles at Shatby and Mustapha Kamel and stylised Ionic porticoes, also at Mustapha Kamel (figure 2). The use of the Greek orders indicates that these tombs probably belonged to families of immigrants who came to Alexandria in the first wave of settlers. The walls are decorated in an architectonic scheme of painting, which has undergone stylistic development throughout the period, from a simple masonry style at Shatby, to the use of blocks of colour incorporating stippling, marbling and incision, imitating stone revetments in porphyry and alabaster, as at Mustapha Kamel (figure 3). The owner of a sumptuous

3. Reconstruction drawing of architectonic decoration incorporating a loculus closure slab in the form of a false door, Chamber 7, Tomb 1, Necropolis of Mustapha Kamel, Alexandria (mid third to early second century BC). (After Adriani)

4. Burial chamber of the Alabaster Tomb, Latin Cemeteries, Alexandria (early third century BC).

5. Architectonic paintwork, Necropolis of Anfushy, Alexandria: (a) Chamber 3, Hypogeum 3; (b) showing change of decoration in Chamber 1, Hypogeum 2 – first phase (ashlar style), second century BC; second phase (tile design), late first century BC. (After Adriani. Graphics courtesy of Derek Edwards)

a   b

burial chamber, the so-called Alabaster Tomb (figure 4), could afford the real thing, as it is constructed entirely of monolithic blocks of grained calcite. The opulence of the tomb confirms high-status ownership and has led to its consideration as a possible burial place of Alexander the Great. Architectonic paintwork has been further elaborated into a zone-style, with courses of simulated ashlar masonry on the upper part of the wall, in the Sidi Gaber, Mafrousa, Gabbari and Anfushy tombs (figure 5), and incorporating relief cutting in the Gabbari necropolis. This 'masonry' style also has its roots in the Greek Hellenistic tradition of public, domestic and funerary architecture. The *oikos*-type Anfushy tombs on Pharos Island (third century to mid first century BC) contain a

6. Chamber 1, Hypogeum 2, Necropolis of Anfushy, Alexandria, showing imitation tile decoration and sculpted portal to burial chamber (late first century BC). (Courtesy of Robert Partridge)

profusion of architectonic paintwork incorporating, towards the end of the second century and the beginning of the first century BC, Egyptianising schemes imitating black and white tiles. The emphasis is now on sculpted portals incorporating Egyptian lotiform pilasters, broken lintels, segmental pediments, friezes of uraei and pedestals for sphinxes (figure 6). In Hypogeum 2 the tilework is interspersed by larger tiles with Egyptian *atef* crowns and, in the lunettes of the entrance staircase, two scenes from the Egyptian funerary repertoire have been added, showing the deceased in the presence of Osiris. The use of uraei and *atef* crowns is interesting. Formerly the prerogative of royalty in the Pharaonic Period, these motifs have now been appropriated for persons of a non-royal status.

Although the size and opulence of these tombs indicate the social standing of the deceased, personal details remain elusive. Tomb 1, Mustapha Kamel, however, gives a rare clue. A figured frieze in the peristyle portrays three cavalrymen and two standing female figures, all turning towards an altar (figure 7). The central rider may be the deceased, the female figures priestesses, and the scene may symbolise part of the funerary ceremonies. Evidence that cult activity took place within the tombs is provided by chambers for the storage of cult items, wells for

7. (Above) Reproduction of painted frieze, Tomb 1, Necropolis of Mustapha Kamel, Alexandria (mid third to second century BC). (After Adriani) (Below) Painted frieze now reconstructed *in situ* over central portal of peristyle court. (Courtesy of Dr Peter Dixon. Graphics courtesy of Derek Edwards)

the supply of water for the ritual, and central altars. In technique, the paint was applied on a layer of plaster and the general outline washed on in fresco. The details in dark red, purple, yellow, pink and blue were then added as the plaster dried, resulting in a tempera effect. The artist has achieved a sense of urgency and movement by using different postures, the horses rearing up to the right in three-quarter foreshortened view and their riders turning towards the left. This verve contrasts sharply with the calm, pious posture of the female figures. During this early Ptolemaic Period Alexandria would have been heavily populated with military personnel and this tomb was probably intended for one of the high-status military families in the city. Illusionistic devices and surprise elements are a feature of the tombs, such as false windows at Shatby and the naturalistic and impressionistic representation of a grove or garden intended to be seen as if beyond a *trompe l'oeil* portico at Anfushy (figure 8).

Unique rural scenes occur in the Painted Tomb from Wardiyan (second century BC). The principal scene depicts an arbour with trellis and climbing foliage, beneath which two oxen turn a *saqqiyeh* attended by a young boy playing pan-pipes (figure 9). The water source is represented below by a pool with waterfowl. Important art-historical considerations here are the simulation of recession and perspective, movement, depth and cast shadows and by the almost impressionistic technique. An adjacent scene of a herm of Pan in a woodland setting is painted in the

8. Reconstruction drawing of niche decoration in the form of a stylised portico with sacred grove beyond, above a sarcophagus painted to represent a bier cloth; Chamber 2, Hypogeum 5, Necropolis of Anfushy, Alexandria (late first century BC). (After Adriani. Graphics courtesy of Derek Edwards)

9. Rural scene showing oxen working a *saqqiyeh*, from the Painted Tomb from Wardiyan (probably mid to late second century BC), now relocated to the Graeco-Roman Museum, Alexandria.

same style, as also is a pastoral scene of a shepherd carrying an animal on his shoulders. Interpreted by some as the Good Shepherd of Christian iconography, a first-century AD date has been suggested and the style of painting resembles that of Pompeiian Style III of similar date. However, accompanying architectonic decoration akin to that in the Anfushy tombs implies the earlier date, in which case the figure is more likely to represent Hermes Psychopompos and the scenes may be termed 'sacral-idyllic'.

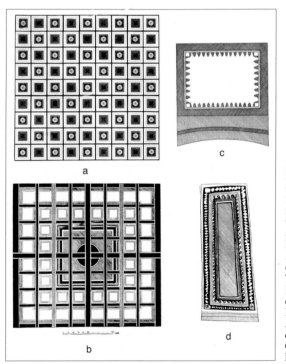

10. Ceiling decoration in Ptolemaic hypogea; (a) burial chamber, Tomb of Mafrousa (second century BC), formerly Eastern Necropolis, now relocated to the garden of the Graeco-Roman Museum, Alexandria; (b) burial chamber 2, Hypogeum 2, Necropolis of Anfushy, Alexandria (late first century BC); (c) niche ceiling, Tomb 3, Necropolis of Mustapha Kamel, Alexandria (third to second century BC); (d) Loculus, Hypogeum 5, Necropolis of Anfushy, Alexandria (late first century BC). (All after Adriani. Graphics courtesy of Derek Edwards)

16

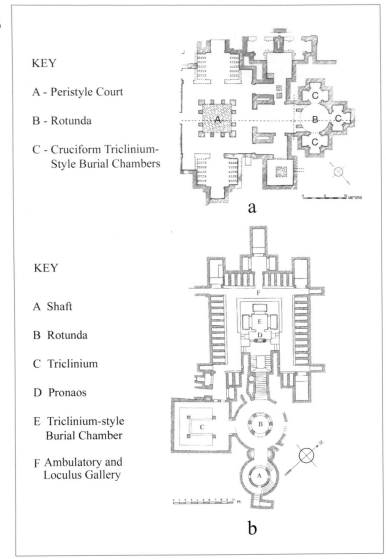

KEY

A - Peristyle Court

B - Rotunda

C - Cruciform Triclinium-
    Style Burial Chambers

a

KEY

A Shaft

B Rotunda

C Triclinium

D Pronaos

E Triclinium-style
   Burial Chamber

F Ambulatory and
   Loculus Gallery

b

11. Plans of triclinium tombs: (a) Grand Hypogeum of Wardiyan, Alexandria (late first century BC to early first century AD), with peristyle court and triclinium-form burial chambers; (b) plan of the Catacombs of Kom el-Shugafa, Alexandria (first to early second century AD). (Both after Adriani. Graphics courtesy of Derek Edwards)

Ceiling and vault decoration also contributes to the concept of illusionism in these tombs, with a profusion of geometric designs and *trompe l'oeil* effects to imitate coffers, and some interior niches are decorated to simulate textiles, awnings and canopies (figure 10).

12. Sculpted portico to the pronaos fronting the principal burial chamber, Kom el-Shugafa, Alexandria, showing columns of mixed style, sculpted figures of the Agathodaemon and Medusa heads flanking the entrance to the burial chamber. Shell relief in the rotunda (first to second century AD). (Courtesy of Robert Partridge)

At the end of the Ptolemaic Period burial chambers took the form of a *triclinium* with three sarcophagi positioned at right angles, and this became the standard form in tombs of the Imperial Period (figure 11).

Eclecticism reached its zenith in the first century AD when Greek and Roman features were combined with Egyptianising elements into a truly mixed style, exemplified by the reliefs in the Kom el-Shugafa 'catacomb' in Alexandria (first to second century AD) – a vast funerary complex on three levels, with rotunda and triclinium on the first level, principal burial chamber on the second level and rows of subsequently cut loculi and sarcophagi on the second and third levels, all accessed by a deep shaft and spiral staircase. It was originally a family tomb, and the plan of the nucleus on the second level follows the concept of a Greek temple with a surrounding ambulatory providing access to the points of interment at the back. The portico to the pronaos comprises rock-cut columns and pilasters with Egyptianising papyriform bases and capitals with mixed acanthus and lotus buds (figure 12). The reliefs flanking the entrance to the burial chamber are also of mixed iconography. Greek Medusa heads are combined with cobras representing Serapis-Agathodaemon wearing Egyptian crowns but also holding the caduceus and thyrsus of Hermes and Dionysus, and Anubis is dressed and equipped as a Roman soldier (figure 13). All protect the tomb and personify victory over the enemies of the dead. Flanking the entrance to the burial chamber are niches with statues representing the tomb owners, combining Egyptian pose with Greek naturalistic heads and Roman hairstyles (figure 14). The burial chamber is triclinium in form. Within, there is a similar amalgam of iconography, including Egyptian funerary subjects – the deceased on leonine bier attended by Anubis (figure 15), presentation of a *wesekh* collar to the Apis Bull and

13. (a) Sculpted figure of the Agathodaemon wearing an Egyptian crown and holding the wands of Hermes and Dionysus; Medusa head above; exterior of walls flanking the entrance to burial chamber. (b) Figure of Anubis dressed as Hermanubis; interior of the same walls; Kom el-Shugafa, Alexandria. (Courtesy of Dr Peter Dixon and Robert Partridge)

scenes which may represent rites of initiation into the cult of Isis, which had, by now, become popular throughout the Mediterranean world. The artist seems to have been more familiar with the Greek elements as these are executed with more skill than the Egyptian ones and glaring errors of interpretation occur. For example, only three Canopic jars are

shown (figure 15) and hieroglyphic inscriptions are unintelligible. In the rotunda are benches within *arcosolia* in the form of cockle-shells, an Alexandrian innovation and seen in other tombs of the period. The complex was subsequently enlarged to incorporate galleries of loculi and may have passed into the hands of one of the burial guilds prevalent in the Roman period.

Decoration in the Tigrane Tomb (early first century AD) is in the mixed style in the painted medium. Narrative scenes of death, resurrection and

14. One of two statues, possibly representing the tomb owners, in niches flanking the entrance to the burial chamber, Catacombs of Kom el-Shugafa, Alexandria (first century AD). (After Von Bissing. Graphics courtesy of Derek Edwards)

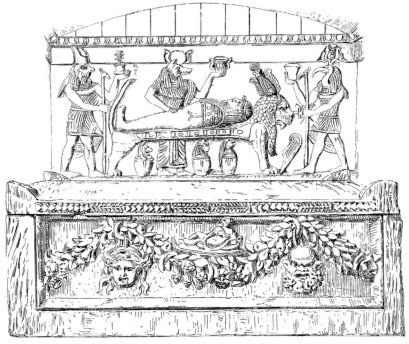

15. Central *arcosolium*, Kom el-Shugafa; Anubis attending the mummiform deceased above the classically decorated principal sarcophagus in the burial chamber; Catacombs of Kom el-Shugafa, Alexandria (first century AD). (After Von Bissing. Graphics courtesy of Derek Edwards)

16. Burial chamber of the Tigrane Tomb, relocated to Kom el-Shugafa gardens, Alexandria; painted scene, representing death and mummification, above the sarcophagus in the central *arcosolium* (mid second century AD). (Courtesy of Robert Partridge)

apotheosis occur which may be interpreted either as extracts from the myth of Osiris or rites of Isis, both representing rebirth after death. The deceased is represented firstly mummiform (figure 16), in the rhomboidal wrappings typical of Roman Period mummies, on his bier (now no longer leonine but a purely Roman structure) and attended by Isis and Nephthys; secondly, as he is reborn, discarding his wrappings under the tutelage of the two goddesses; and thirdly, as he kneels before Isis. Anubis is present but relegated to a side pillar. Architectonic work is present in the painted piers, decorated to represent stylised Roman columns, and in the dome-shaped ceiling, which simulates a ribbed vault with an *oculus* through which peers a Greek Medusa head.

Also decorated in the painted medium, the Persephone Tombs within the Kom el-Shugafa catacomb complex reveal a double use of styles in the principal *arcosolium* – the upper registers showing a formal representation of Anubis attending to the mummy of the deceased, and the lower registers depicting the abduction of Persephone by Hades in the much freer and more spontaneous Greek style. Both scenes symbolise rebirth and victory over death, Persephone here being associated with Isis. Similarly, the Shounat Stagni burial chamber has painted scenes personifying Isis-Aphrodite and the goddess Nemesis, who was also concerned with the protection of the dead and associated with Isis.

Alexandria's cemeteries are all situated under the spread of the modern city and consequently tomb superstructures have been destroyed. However, evidence from some of the settlements to the west of the city confirms the existence of above-ground structures over similar tomb types.

a

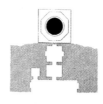

b

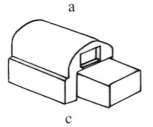

c

17. Tomb plans, north coast and Delta cemeteries. (a) Hypogeum 1, Necropolis of Plinthine (third to second century BC). (After Adriani) (b) Rock-cut tomb superimposed by a stone tower in the form of a Pharos, Taposiris Magna (late first century BC). (After Voros) (c) Reconstruction of brick-built tomb with niche for emplacement of stela, Necropolis of Terenouthis (Kom Abu-Billou) (third to fourth century AD). (After Wagner. Graphics courtesy of Derek Edwards)

North coast settlements and Nile Delta (figure 17)

The cemeteries of Plinthine, Taposiris Magna, Marina el-Alamein, Mersa Matruh and Zawiyet umm el-Rakham lie along the north coast ridge and reveal both similarities to and variations of those of the capital. Rock-cut tombs and hypogea with loculi, open courts and peristyles exist at Plinthine (figure 17a) and Mersa Matruh, and at Plinthine walled areas enclose family tombs. Triclinium tombs also occur at Plinthine and at Taposiris Magna; one such tomb is superimposed by a tower shaped as a scaled-down replica of the Pharos in Alexandria (figure 17b). At Marina el-Alamein some above-ground structures consist of stone-built, cube-shaped chambers with loculi. Others comprise simple trenches covered by rectangular prisms of sand and small stones contained within vertical limestone slabs. Larger pillar tombs occur (figure 18), some superimposed by columns up to 7 metres high and topped with protruding entablatures, cornices, Nabataean-style capitals and sometimes a funerary sculpture of the deceased in reclining posture. Hypogea exist, accessed by rock-cut dromoi leading to open courts with light-wells preceding the tomb nucleii. The burial chambers contain two large *klinai*, on which the deceased would have been placed side by side, and evidence exists for loculus burials. Portals present evidence of stylised acanthus capital decoration. Two hypogea have above-ground multi-chambered structures that may have served as pavilions in which the funerary ceremonies, banquets and ritual activities took place. Mummies found in one of these larger tombs indicate that

18. Reconstructed pillar tombs, Necropolis of Marina el-Alamein (second century BC to third century AD).

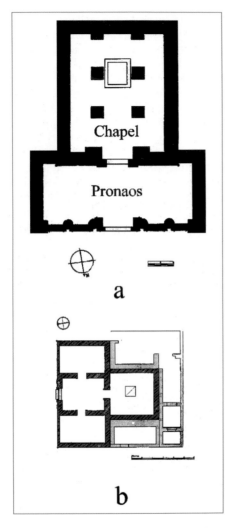

19. Nile Valley tomb plans. (a) Tomb of Petosiris (late fourth to early third century BC), Tuna el-Gebel. (After Lefebvre) (b) Funerary House 21 (first to second century AD), Tuna el-Gebel. (After Gabra. Graphics courtesy of Derek Edwards)

the pavilions may also have been used for their display before interment in the chambers below, thus contributing to theories that mummies of the period were kept above ground.

The majority of Graeco-Roman sites in the Delta await excavation but the cemetery at Kom Abu-Billou (ancient Terenouthis) (late third century/early fourth century AD) has revealed mudbrick tombs consisting of no less than twenty-four types, the most popular being mastaba-shaped structures with barrel vaults (figure 17c) or truncated pyramidal-shaped roofs, coated in stucco and decorated in fresco technique with designs incorporating Alexandrian-style geometric, floral and fauna motifs. Niches in the eastern façades held the 'Terenouthis' stelae discussed in Chapter 3, fronted by separate mudbrick offering tables. Few burials were found actually within the tombs, the human remains being interred around them, which lends to the theory that the tomb structures were family cenotaphs or places for enactment of the ritual.

The Nile Valley

It is in the Nile Valley that Graeco-Roman funerary contexts have suffered most, but what remains indicates an eclectic mix of Greek, Roman and Egyptian styles and beliefs. Hundreds of simple pit tombs occur throughout. At Hawara in the Fayum, a range of rough burial pits have, in contrast to their simplicity, yielded magnificent mummies with masks and portraits. Other tombs there reveal remains of mudbrick tomb chapels with benches and niches for coffin emplacements and, at Er-Rubayat, a circular 'hall' surrounded by several burial chambers. Burials occur in age-old funerary complexes such as Saqqara, where the deceased of whatever status could benefit from the sacredness of the site. Concentrations of burials also occur around the seats of religious importance such as Denderah and Akhmim, as attested by mummy labels detailing the name, place of residence and destination of the body. At Abydos tombs dating from the late Ptolemaic Period into the Roman Period, and associated with the sculptural relief stelae discussed in Chapter 3, range from simple pits to tombs with mudbrick superstructures in the form of mastabas, sarcophagi or barrel vaulted chambers (figure 47). One tomb is recorded as having painted scenes of the deceased in the presence of Osiris, Isis, Nephthys, Horus and Thoth.

Extensive Graeco-Roman cemeteries have been excavated at Qau el-Kebir, revealing burials beneath small, square brick-built structures with interior niches. The walls were painted white and sometimes decorated with a figure of the tomb owner in Roman style and dress. Re-use of earlier tombs and structures became prevalent, for example at Deir el-Medina, where two generations of a priestly family of the late second century AD were interred in the cellar of a house, the place of burial sometimes appearing to be of lesser importance than the body, which became a 'burial' entity in itself, and in Thebes the Soter family were interred in a tomb of the Ramesside Period.

At Athribis, near Sohag, two types of rock-cut tomb have been identified: the *shaft* type, for example the tomb of Psenosiris, mayor of Athribis in the early first century AD, entirely decorated in sunk relief with scenes of Egyptian iconography; and the *façade* type, for example the tomb of Mery-Hor. This tomb has painted scenes from the Egyptian repertoire – mythological figures leading the deceased in the underworld, the deceased on a bier being mourned by Isis and adoring the goddesses of the hours – and also indicates a renaissance in funerary astrological beliefs in the Imperial Period with 'zodiac' ceilings representing the horoscopes of the deceased and his father, dating to *c*.AD 140 (figure 20). Greek astronomical signs are combined with Egyptian figures and *Ba*-birds representing the souls of the deceased surrounded by signs of the mansions of the moon.

At Akhmim (ancient Panopolis) tomb types at El-Salamuni consist of vertical shaft tombs, single rock-cut chamber tombs and larger hypogea with niches for emplacement of the deceased. Several have coarsely painted decoration in a mixed style with friezes of Egyptian narrative scenes – processions of gods and the barque of the sun-god, above

24

20. Reproduction of Zodiac Ceiling A, the Zodiac Tomb, Athribis, near Sohag, Upper Egypt (*c*.AD 140). (After Petrie)

architectonic panels in the Alexandrian style, and large-scale depictions of the deceased dressed in a Roman toga and holding a papyrus roll, to demonstrate his educated status. Some ceilings are painted with circular zodiacs, for example Tomb 3A, in which twelve segments surround a central figure of Isis-Sothis. Four goddesses are depicted in the corners as if supporting the zodiac.

Excavations at Antinoopolis have revealed tumuli in the shape of brick or stone plinths superimposed by rectangular structures with burial pits beneath. More wealthy burials incorporate tomb chapels having single or double chambers, with *arcosolia* and decoration with floral and geometric motifs imitating intarsia and architectonic paintwork in the Alexandrian style. The best-preserved decoration of this type can be seen in the cemetery of Tuna el-Gebel grouped around the tomb of Petosiris, who, like his father and brother before him, was High Priest of Thoth (assimilated by the Greeks into Hermes). This family held office during the Persian domination of Egypt and the coming of Alexander, and it was through priests like these that administration and control were exercised throughout the Graeco-Roman Period. Petosiris' tomb (late fourth/early third century BC; figure 19a) resembles a small

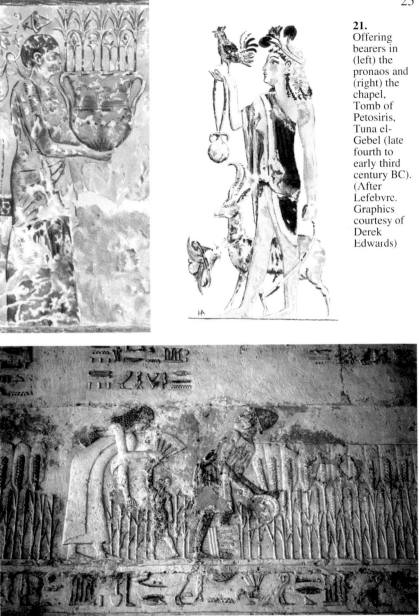

21. Offering bearers in (left) the pronaos and (right) the chapel, Tomb of Petosiris, Tuna el-Gebel (late fourth to early third century BC). (After Lefebvre. Graphics courtesy of Derek Edwards)

22. Scene of work in the fields; pronaos, east wall, upper register, Tomb of Petosiris, Tuna el-Gebel (late fourth to early third century BC). (Courtesy of Robert Partridge)

23. Scene of sacrifice with the family grouped around a shrine-shaped tomb; pronaos, south wall, east side, lower register, Tomb of Petosiris, Tuna el-Gebel (late fourth to early third century BC). (After Lefebvre)

Egyptian temple, with stone-built chapel incorporating pillared pronaos, naos and underground burial chambers. The art in this tomb reflects the early grafting of Greek artistic conventions on to Egyptian funerary decoration in this important religious centre. The interior of the chapel is decorated with scenes in the Egyptian tradition – Petosiris paying homage to his father and brother, the Opening of the Mouth ceremony and the presentation of offerings. In the pronaos, on the other hand, the registers of offering bearers (figure 21) and genre scenes (figure 22) reveal a subtle change of style – the figures are rendered naturalistically and personalised with individual features, and the three-quarter and frontal poses give an impression of depth. The colour palette is different, too. The figures wear contemporary dress in light shades and the rendering of the drapery gives a sense of volume. Also in the pronaos is a wholly Greek scene of sacrifice and of the family grouped around the tomb, represented as a cupboard shrine with the doors of the upper panels ajar (figure 23).

By the second century AD this tomb had become the focus for pilgrimages and around it a large cemetery of brick- and stone-built tomb chapels imitating contemporary housing had grown up serving the settlement of Hermopolis Magna (figure 19b). Many are undecorated but the exterior façades of some chapels imitate ashlar

24. Tomb chapel of Ptolemaios, Tuna el-Gebel (late first century BC to second century AD). (Courtesy of Robert Partridge)

25. Reproduction of architectonic decoration, Tuna el-Gebel (late first century BC to second century AD). (After Gabra)

masonry incorporating Egyptianising pilasters and illusionistic Greek-style false 'windows' (figure 24), and some were originally decorated with geometric motifs and pictorial designs. Interiors are painted in architectonic style but now with more elaborate panels revealing similarities to Pompeian Style II (figure 25). An amalgam of subject matter is present – genre scenes, mythological subjects, floral decoration and shell motifs. Analysis of names reveals devotees of a variety of cults, such as Isis, Thoth/Hermes and Osiris, and the prominence of the combined cult of Osiris/Dionysus is evident in the representation of cult objects. Crude decoration of vines interspersed with scenes of childbirth invokes fecundity. Scenes of Greek mythology occur, including the popular funerary theme of the Abduction of Persephone (figure 26). In House 21 (figure 19b), the upper parts of walls are entirely covered with painted registers of scenes of traditional Egyptian derivation, above a dado of Greek architectonic decoration simulating veined marble plaques and mosaic tesserae. The deceased is represented in both contemporary and traditional Egyptian costume, firstly being anointed by Horus and Thoth with the water of purification, and secondly in a scene of adoration. In both, she is accompanied by a rare depiction of her shadow (figure 27). Inscriptions give an indication of occupations such as horse-breeders, administrators, gymnasium masters and purveyors of fine linen from the nearby town of Hermopolis Magna.

26. Reproduction of a painted scene of the Abduction of Persephone, Funerary House 16, Tuna el-Gebel (late first century BC to second century AD). (After Gabra)

27. Reproduction scenes of the deceased dressed (left) in contemporary costume and (right) in traditional Egyptian style; Funerary House 21, Tuna el-Gebel (second century AD). (After Gabra. Graphics courtesy of Derek Edwards)

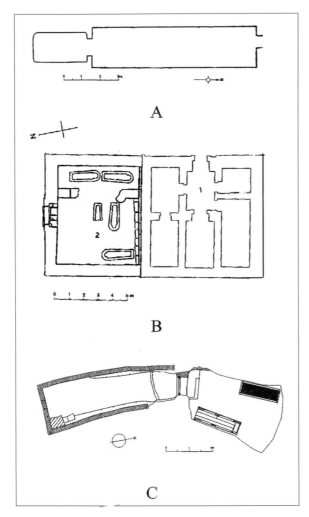

28. Tomb plans, oases cemeteries. (a) Tomb of Si-Amun, Gebel Mawta, Siwa Oasis (late fourth to early third century BC). (After Fakhri) (b) Tomb 1 (of Kitines) and Tomb 2, Ezbet Bashendi, Dakhleh Oasis (late first century BC to early first century AD). (After Yamani) (c) Dromos Tomb 6, with stretcher biers *in situ*, Necropolis of Douch, Kharga Oasis (first to fourth century AD). (After Dunand *et al.* Graphics courtesy of Derek Edwards)

The oases

During the Roman Period military outposts protecting the trade routes of the Western Desert led to expansion of the settlements in the oases. A variety of types of burial can be observed, ranging from simple rectangular rock-cut pits to larger chamber tombs cut in rocky outcrops and in the desert cliffs, as in Siwa (figure 28a), El-Bahrein and El-Areg; family tombs with entrance dromoi, niches, side chambers and *klinai*, as in Bahariya; tombs accessed by rock-cut staircases leading to chambers

29. Scene from the Tomb of Si-Amun, Siwa Oasis, showing the tomb owner in contemporary dress and hairstyle (late fourth century to early third century BC). (Courtesy of Derek Edwards)

with superimposed rows of loculi, for example in Siwa; monumental stone-built mastaba-type structures, as in Dakhleh (figure 28b); and rock-cut chambers accessed by either a vertical shaft or open-air dromos-type descending corridor, as in Kharga (figure 28c).

The Siwan tomb of Si-Amun dates to the late fourth/early third century BC. The tomb owner and his family are portrayed in the usual Egyptian scenes such as the Weighing of the Heart, the Opening of the Mouth ceremony and the adoration of deities. What is different is the manner in which some of the figures have been portrayed individualistically. Si-Amun is depicted with fair skin, a black beard and contemporary hairstyle (figure 29). His elder son is also of light complexion and wears contemporary dress, whereas his wife and younger son are dark-skinned. The style is coarse, however, and may reflect influence from Cyrene rather than directly from Greece. The ceiling is based on Egyptian motifs and iconography with a representation of the sky goddess Nut and the journey of the solar barque in the vault of heaven.

In the Dakhleh Oasis, the remains of six stone-built, mastaba-shaped monumental tombs about 7.5 metres square (late first century BC/early first century AD) are situated in the village of Bashendi. Best preserved

30. Scene from the Tomb of Petosiris, Qaret el-Muza-waqa, Dakhleh Oasis, showing the tomb owner in contemporary Roman dress (late first to second century AD). (Courtesy of Derek Edwards)

are Tomb 1, the tomb of Kitines, which has a flat roof and Egyptian relief decoration, and Tomb 4, which has a domed roof and decorative pilasters with stylised classical bases and capitals, all preserved inside the later Ottoman tomb of Sheikh Bashendi. They are evidence of the wealth and significance of this settlement in Roman times. A mixed style is also seen in Dakhleh in the painted decoration of the tombs of Petubastis (first century AD) and Petosiris (early second century AD) at Qaret el-Muzawaqa. Traditional Egyptian funerary motifs are adopted – the mummy lying on the bier, attended by Anubis, Isis and Nephthys, the Weighing of the Heart ceremony and scenes of libation, but the manner in which they have been executed is different and the style has degenerated into badly proportioned figures that are a parody of their earlier Egyptian counterparts. The figure of the tomb owner, Petosiris, is shown large-scale following Egyptian convention (figure 30), but his dress is Roman and his three-quarter posture follows Greek artistic tradition, as does the technique – colour washes punctuated by darker lines to give an effect of movement and shading. The central figure making offerings is also in frontal position with the left leg bent at the knee, while that on the right is in more typical Egyptian posture.

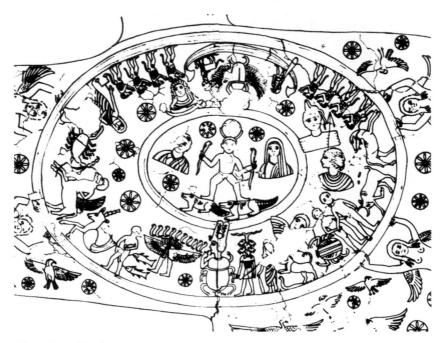

31. Zodiac ceiling from the Tomb of Petosiris, Qaret el-Muzawaqa, Dakhleh Oasis (late first to second century AD). (After Parker, in Osing *et al*)

A significant form of decoration in these tombs is the vine motif, symbolising fecundity and representing the importance of viticulture in the oases at this time. Zodiac ceilings like those of El-Salamuni also occur: for example, in the first chamber of the tomb of Petosiris the signs are arranged clockwise, surrounded by a double-headed *ourobouros* and supported by four winged goddesses representing the cardinal points. In the centre are personifications of the planets and northern constellations. In the inner chamber, the central figure is of Horus standing on two crocodiles and grasping snakes (figure 31). Both ceilings represent the escape of the soul, assisted by the sun, moon and planets and protected from evil forces.

Bringing the period to a close, the extensive cemetery of El-Bagawat in the Kharga Oasis consists of some ten different types of brick-built tomb chapels, ranging from simple single-chambered structures to more complex ones with domes, apses and barrel vaults. Many are undecorated but architectonic paintwork is present in some, together with important early Christian scenes in the Chapel of the Exodus and the Chapel of Peace; these are significant in the study of early Christian art but are outside the scope of this book.

3
Loculus slabs and funerary stelae

Loculus slabs

In Alexandria and the north coast settlements, where the dead were deposited in loculi or niches (figure 32), many apertures were closed with limestone slabs decorated in red, blue and yellow to resemble double doors set within a framework of painted stucco (figure 33), complementing the architectonic work in the tombs (figure 3). The style derives from Hellenistic originals but the technique is fresco, in contrast to secco of similar examples from Greece. The upper sections of many panels are painted to imitate a grille or trellis with foliage and garlands. Optical illusion is present where the cross-bars, jambs and entablatures are carved in relief or formed of applied stucco, causing the panels to appear recessed, and by nail-heads, handles and doorknobs, all simulated in paint. The effect is increased by light and shade effects in the 'grilles' of the upper panels, and the illusion of being able to see beyond the door is

32. (Left) Rock-cut loculi, Necropolis of Gabbari, Alexandria.

33. (Below) Types of false door from the Necropolis of Hadra, Alexandria (early third to mid second century BC). (After Adriani)

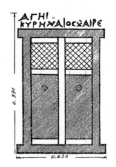

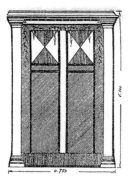

34. Loculus closure slab in the form of an Egyptianising false door set within a Classical framework (Roman Period); from Mersa Matruh.

accentuated by the spaces being painted blue, implying open air beyond. These are not false doors in the Egyptian sense. In Greek funerary beliefs, the soul did not return to partake of offerings in the Egyptian tradition. It is perhaps better to consider them as the doors through which the soul could be released. This is sometimes confirmed by a *dexiosis* scene, two figures clasping hands painted on the door panels, and by inscriptions giving the name of the deceased, a valediction and a salutation, such as 'Athinaia, worthy, farewell'. Into the Roman Period, style and decoration follow the Egyptianising trends present in the tomb decoration, with motifs such as the use of the broken lintel and frieze of uraei in combination with classical elements such as Doric column shafts (figure 34).

Hellenistic stelae

A series of figured limestone stelae, originally affixed to grave markers or loculus apertures, comes from Alexandria and the cemeteries of the north coast. Two classes exist – painted sculptural and painted free-style. A varied colour palette has been used, applied using tempera or gouache technique, giving a sense of vivacity to the figures. The subject matter is the same for both classes – single figures or groups of figures. Hand-clasp (*dexiosis*) scenes frequently occur (figure 35), deriving from Greek Classical and Hellenistic stelae. Many represent the military men of the city, either with their families or in action. Interesting postures have been possible in the painted medium. Warriors are depicted in the

35. Hellenistic stela, sculptural class, showing *dexiosis* (mid third century BC). (Graeco-Roman Museum, Alexandria: GRM 24093)

prime of life, standing loosely in three-quarter frontal positions and captured in a moment of activity, turning to look at their family members (figure 36), or in the act of launching a spear. Cavalrymen are also included in the repertoire, with vigorous action scenes of horse and rider in motion (figure 37), similar to the frieze in Tomb 1, Mustapha Kamel. The artist has attempted to resolve many technical problems – the movement and musculature of the straining animal, the braking action of the horseman and the effects of light and shade. Dating is based on inscriptions which give only the name, a valediction and a salutation, and on stylistic development, from the

36. Reproduction of a Hellenistic stela, painted class, showing a warrior with children (mid third century BC); original from Necropolis of Shatby. (Graeco-Roman Museum, Alexandria. After Breccia)

37. Reproduction of a Hellenistic stela, painted class, portraying a cavalryman and squire (mid third century BC); original from Necropolis of Shatby. (Graeco-Roman Museum, Alexandria: GRM 10228. After Breccia)

static, large-scale figures of the earliest examples to the loose-limbed and lively postures of the more accomplished ones. The series then declines into linear and stiff postures until in the Roman Period the figures are represented in static, frontal positions, sometimes set within Egyptianising portals or temple-type façades composed of columns with

composite capitals and entablatures of uraei and winged scarabs (figure 38).

Interpretation of the scenes is not as easy as it might seem. For example, what do the hand-clasp scenes represent? Where is the action taking place – in this world or the next? Is the *dexiosis* a farewell or a greeting? Do they represent the deceased being welcomed by other dead? Or is the deceased taking leave of his loved ones? The feeling of sadness and reverential awe which these stelae inspire would tend towards this last interpretation. Do inscriptions help? Yes, but only in limited fashion,

38. Sculpted stela of a figure in an Egyptianising portal (Roman Period); from the Necropolis of Gabbari. (Graeco-Roman Museum, Alexandria: GRM 3215)

39. Hieroglyphic stela from Edfu (late first century BC to first century AD). (Museum of Egyptian Antiquities, Cairo: 22018. After Kamal)

because only one name is indicated and where pairs of figures exist the name cannot be attributed to any particular one. The ethnic origin or family background of the deceased is sometimes indicated – for example 'Polydorus, Thessalian', 'Bitos, son of Lostoiekos' or 'Isidora, Cyrenaean', confirming the multi-racial aspect of Ptolemaic Alexandria and its environs. Symbolically, the stelae are intended to represent and perpetuate the virtues of the deceased. The soldiers' guise represents heroisation, bravery and triumph over death. The women are generally represented in calm postures implying the piety and patience of Persephone, and one represents Isis-Nemesis.

Hieroglyphic relief stelae (figure 39)

Found in cemeteries of provincial towns such as Aswan, Elephantine, Edfu, Luxor, Abydos, Akhmim and Saqqara, and ranging in date from the beginning of the Ptolemaic Period into the Roman Period, these stelae, mainly of limestone, follow the traditional round-topped form of Egyptian precedents. The decoration likewise has its origin in Egyptian funerary motifs and, unlike the Alexandrian stelae, presents little evidence of hellenising influence, either in style or subject matter. Divided into three sections by incised or painted lines, the figures and other motifs have been cut in sunk relief and brightly painted. The standard form of decoration for the upper section, or lunette, is a winged solar disk, uraei and recumbent jackals representing Anubis. The pictorial area below the disk holds themes from the standard Egyptian funerary repertoire – the deceased adoring Osiris accompanied by Isis and Nephthys, and sometimes by the particular patron deity of the city or nome. Other scenes occur of the deceased adoring the barque of the sun-god Ra or, more rarely, the mummy reposing on its bier attended by Anubis, Horus, Isis and Nephthys. The figures and their embellishment follow Egyptian methods of representation. Block colours are used, with no attempt at shading. Red predominates, with black, blue, yellow and green, and some stelae may have been gilded. The lower section is taken up with rows of hieroglyphic inscriptions giving the names of the deities portrayed, the name, titles and affiliation of the deceased, and prayers to the local deity or a hymn to the sun-god. A series of similarly decorated wooden stelae also exists. Uniformity of style makes dating and stylistic development difficult to assess. During the Ptolemaic Period there was no pressure to change local burial customs, but those from the more hellenised settlements such as Akhmim or sites of religious importance, like Abydos and Edfu, are more accomplished than those from, say, Aswan.

Sculptural stelae from Upper Egypt (figure 40)

A series of more hellenised limestone stelae begins in the late first century BC and runs to the beginning of the fourth century AD. Particular find sites are Abydos, Coptos and Denderah, with a few from other areas. Like the hieroglyphic relief stelae, they are divided into three sections and carved mainly in sunk relief and incised, and the same five block colours and method of application are used. In contrast, however, they now portray distinctly Graeco-Roman features alongside purely Egyptian ones. The lunette is decorated with the usual winged sun-disk,

40. Sculptural stela from Abydos (late first century BC), showing the deceased in the company of Osiris, Anubis and Nephthys. (University of Liverpool: E89. Courtesy of School of Archaeology, Classics and Egyptology, University of Liverpool)

pendant uraei and confronted jackals. Sometimes the funerary barque with mummy is shown, signifying the journey to the tomb. The pictorial register contains scenes of the Egyptian funerary repertoire: the deceased being presented by Anubis to Osiris, burning incense, making offerings or gestures of adoration to Osiris and the deities in his entourage, or reposing on his bier. Sometimes family members are present. There is now a distinct change in the manner in which the deceased is depicted. The gods are still rendered in Egyptian manner and posture whereas the deceased and members of his family are shown frontally or in three-quarter view, wear Greek dress and have Greek hairstyles, and the artist has attempted to portray the individual features of the deceased, particularly the head, more naturalistically and with more care. The lower section contains inscriptions in Greek or Demotic, painted or incised, and filled with red or black pigment, giving the name of the deceased, his age, affiliation and, more rarely, his profession and sometimes an epithet or prayer. Hieroglyphs, where present, identify the deities present in the pictorial scene, but the overall absence of these in comparison with the hieroglyphic relief stelae is interesting. Only rare glimpses into the professions of the deceased are given – for example 'gardener', 'seller of myrtle berries', 'embalmer'. Very few give a discernible date, that is a regnal year of a particular emperor, and stylistic development is difficult to ascertain, but the earlier examples and those from more hellenised settlements are more accomplished than those from more rural sites. Some also have a dedication to the god Serapis, which is obviously intended to refer to the image of Osiris, and this indicates how widespread the acceptance of the cult had become at the end of the Ptolemaic Period and reveals the extent to which provincial capitals, particularly those around large temple complexes, had become hellenised.

'Terenouthis' stelae (figure 41)

A series of round-topped limestone stelae dating from the late third century to the early fourth century AD comes from various Delta sites, particularly Kom Abu-Billou (ancient Terenouthis). Originally positioned in niches in the exterior walls of brick-built tombs (figure 17c), they portray predominantly standing or reclining figures framed by incised lines or sometimes sculpted columns and entablature. Carved in either sunk or high relief, the details are incised or modelled and painted – in shades of ochre for both sexes and bright colours such as yellow, pink and blue for the dress. The figures are impersonal and uniform in style and dress – Greek chiton and sometimes a himation, with only the hairstyle serving to distinguish the sexes – short curls for the male, and long tresses with centre parting, reminiscent of the Egyptian wig, for the female figures. One wears a diadem, which may have associations

41. 'Terenouthis' stela from the Delta (late third to mid fourth century AD); reclining female figure on couch. (Museum of Egyptian Antiquities, Cairo: 9258. After Milne)

with the cult of Serapis. The erect figures are frontally positioned, with upraised arms, and the reclining figures repose on a couch and hold a libation cup, symbolically participating in the funerary repast and ritual. The ritual items and receptacles are depicted frontally in the Egyptian manner on the façade of the couch.

There are also a few stelae portraying the deceased reclining in a boat, some seated, some groups of figures, and one or two in the act of making a sacrifice. The upraised position of the arms in the standing figures resembles both the *Ka* of Egyptian iconography and the *orans* position of prayer in Christian practice, but neither is likely to be of significance here. The action was a sign of adoration in Dynastic Egypt, frequently used in the Graeco-Roman period and seen inside coffin lids of the period. What we have, rather, is a combination of Greek and Egyptian symbolism. For example, the architectural setting is derived from Attic stelae, but the columns are papyriform, lotiform or Classical in form and the frequent presence of jackals or hawks representing Anubis and Horus are an indication of Egyptian practice, although of course an association of Anubis with Argos would have been an easy step. The figures, too, are a combination of Greek and Egyptian methods of representation. The reclining figure is Greek in style, the banqueting scene and the frontal position of the standing figures are Roman, but the feet are rendered in profile in the Egyptian manner. The figures are static and the feeling of emotion and pathos portrayed in the Hellenistic stelae is absent. Nevertheless, the Graeco-Roman aspect is much stronger than in the stelae from Upper Egypt and the more accomplished ones are more Greek than Egyptian. The presence of boats may represent both the solar boat of Egyptian funerary iconography and the craft which symbolically transported the deceased across the River Styx, a concept confirmed by the presence of coins found in the burials. The lower portion of the stela is inscribed in Greek, giving the name and age of the deceased, an epithet and a salutation, for example, 'Achillas, devoted to his children, about sixty-eight years old, Farewell'. Some also give details of parentage and, rarely, the occupation – linen merchant, purveyor of condiments, carver of hieroglyphs. Dating is done on the basis of a very few inscriptions which give the year of the reigning emperor and day of the month and by analysis of the coins, but stylistic development is difficult to discern. The stelae are testament to the still lingering influence of the local Egyptian culture in an area close to Alexandria after five hundred years or more of foreign occupation.

42

4
Sarcophagi, coffins and body cases

Sarcophagi

Engaged rock-cut *kline* sarcophagi are an integral feature of the Alexandrian hypogea. During the Ptolemaic Period large hollowed-out cavities, divided into compartments for multiple burials, were sculpted and decorated as *klinai* to represent the component parts of the funerary bier – frame, mattresses, cushions and bier cloth (figure 42). They therefore provide valuable information on contemporary types of interior furnishings. Later in the Ptolemaic Period and into the Roman Period the bench or *lenos* type came into use, which could not be accessed from above but were entered via an opening in one of the ends, in the

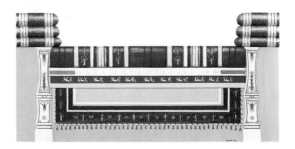

42. (Above) Rock-cut *kline* sarcophagus sculpted in the form of a bier or couch and with painted features representing mattress, pillows and tapestry or bier cloth; Tomb 2, Necropolis of Mustapha Kamel, Alexandria (third century BC). (Below) Reconstruction drawing. (After Adriani)

43. Marble sarcophagus, carved with swags, *erotes*, *nikai*, Medusa and maenad masks (Roman Period); Anfushy Necropolis, Alexandria. (Courtesy of Robert Partridge)

base of the façade or from the back of the chamber. Those of the late Ptolemaic Period, for example in the Ras el-Tin necropolis, present painted geometric designs imitating marble intarsia, and in the triclinium tombs of the Roman Period sculpted decoration predominates, incorporating funerary motifs such as wreaths, garlands and satyrs, Medusa masks and *bucrania*, as at Kom el-Shugafa (figure 15).

Free-standing limestone sarcophagi of this type also occur in Roman Alexandria and bath-sarcophagi in expensive marble and granite are testament to the wealth of the family, as indeed are elaborately carved marble sarcophagi with gabled lids, acroteria and sides sculpted with figures and narrative scenes from Greek mythology (figure 43). Three-dimensional sculptures of the deceased in reclining position grace the lids of some marble sarcophagi.

In the Western Desert, the rock-cut tombs of Douch, Kharga Oasis, have revealed three types of wooden funerary bier: leonine, stuccoed and painted with traditional Egyptian funerary motifs; biers in the form

44. Bath-sarcophagus; Anfushy Necropolis, Alexandria. (Courtesy of Robert Partridge)

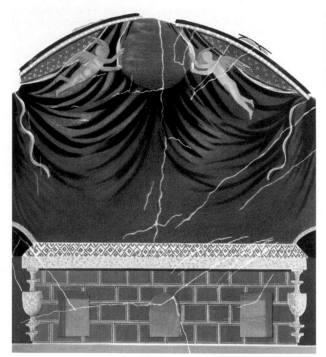

45. *Arcosolium* representing painted *kline* and draped textile with *erotes*; from a funerary house at Tuna el-Gebel (mid to late first century AD). (After Gabra)

of couches painted with figures and garlands in the Alexandrian tradition; and stretcher-type beds made of palm planks secured with palm fibres and used firstly to transport the deceased to the tomb and secondly to serve as the funerary resting place (figure 28c). Simple inhumations also occur where the deceased has been placed on brick or stone supports.

Both in the oases and in the cemeteries serving the Nile Valley, the dead were frequently laid to rest on rock-cut platforms, ledges, niches and *klinai*, some with *arcosolia*, as at Antinoopolis and Akhmim. At Tuna el-Gebel painted funerary couches follow the Alexandrian style (figure 45), resembling free-standing examples with turned legs like that depicted in the Tigrane Tomb (figure 16).

In the provinces the use of huge free-standing sarcophagi is carried through from the second Persian Period into the early Ptolemaic Period. Fashioned of hard stone such as basalt and granite, they are roughly rectangular in shape, slightly narrowing towards the foot and curved at the head. Lids are flat, curved, domed or mansard-shaped. Decoration varies from bands of hieroglyphs, giving the name and titles of the

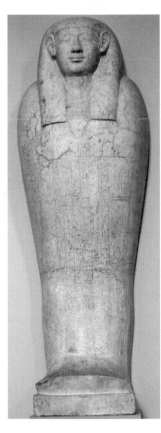

46. Lid of the anthropoid sarcophagus of Padihorhephep; Ptolemaic Period. (Photograph by the author. British Museum: EA790)

deceased, to complex themes and texts from the Egyptian funerary repertoire, covering both the exterior and interior faces. These gave way to large-scale anthropoid stone sarcophagi (figure 46), the breast often engraved with a pectoral decorated with scenes of the deceased on his bier guarded by mourning Isis and Nephthys figures, being re-animated by the rays of the sun-disk and accompanied by jackals indicating the celestial pathway to the afterlife. Vertical lines of texts derived from the Book of the Dead and relating to the acceptance of the deceased in the afterlife are inscribed down the centre of the body, sometimes flanked by images of the four Sons of Horus. Sometimes a human-headed falcon, representing the soul, is shown hovering over the body of the deceased. Human remains were often placed directly into the sarcophagus (figure 47) although more wealthy individuals tended to be buried in an inner coffin, or nests of coffins.

Coffins

In Alexandria dowelled wooden coffins predominate, deposited directly in loculi, niches or inside stone sarcophagi. In Upper Egypt cultural interaction becomes evident in the series of rectangular coffins from provincial cemeteries. Wooden coffins with vaulted lids were adopted in the Ptolemaic Period, with wooden ridge tiles and mouldings and decorated with Greek key motifs. Antefixes of painted stucco, terracotta and wood were sometimes attached, both in the form of Sirens, which in Greek funerary iconography acted as intermediaries between this world and the next, and in the form of protective Medusa masks (figure 48). Coffins with more elaborate lids sporting acroteria occur, decorated with a combination of Greek and Egyptian motifs such as polychrome friezes of Greek egg-and-dart, garland and palmette motifs and *bucrania*, and Egyptian figured compositions (figure 49).

a

b

c

47. (Above) Anthropoid sarcophagi in a brick-lined pit at Abydos (late first century BC to first century AD). (Courtesy of School of Archaeology, Classics and Egyptology, University of Liverpool)

48. (a) Wooden coffin with painted stucco decoration and appliqués, from the Serapeum, Saqqara (late third century BC). (b) Tympanum from the same coffin. (c) Round Medusa plaque from the same coffin. (All, Museum of Egyptian Antiquities, Cairo: 33101, 33102 and 33104. After Edgar. Graphics courtesy of Derek Edwards)

49. Wooden coffin with gabled lid, acroteria and painted stucco decoration; from Nahas in the Fayum (late third century BC). (Museum of Egyptian Antiquities, Cairo: 33123. After Edgar)

Foot   Head

From Thebes comes a series of rectangular wooden coffins with deep lids and baseboards dating to the first/second century AD. The exteriors are highly decorated with scenes of Egyptian funerary iconography, such as the presentation of the deceased to Osiris, the barque of the sun-god towed by jackals, and depictions of the Apis Bull, winged scarabs and protective deities, accompanied by Classical floral and rosette motifs. The interiors of the lids and the baseboards hold representations of the Egyptian sky-goddess Nut – on the lids with arms raised and surrounded by personifications of the hours and signs of the zodiac, and on the baseboards with arms by her side and accompanied by jackals holding the key to the underworld (figure 50). Nut was the mother of Osiris and symbolically here she takes the deceased into her embrace ready to be reborn as Osiris. She is, however, stylistically represented as a Roman lady, wearing contemporary dress and the jewellery which was

50. Wooden baseboard of the coffin of Cornelius, decorated with a figure of Nut below a winged scarab and flanked at the head by images of Isis and Nephthys and at the feet by guardian jackals. Soter burials, Thebes. (Photograph by the author. British Museum: EA 6950)

51. Coffin in the form of a shrine with upper 'barn' doors, in which the mummy could be stored upright and displayed by opening the upper panels in order to receive offerings or participate in family events; from Abusir el-Meleq; Ptolemaic Period (mummy earlier). (Staatliche Museen, Ägyptische Abteilung, Berlin: 17039/40. Graphics courtesy of Derek Edwards)

fashionable during the late first century AD. She nevertheless sports a particularly luxuriant Egyptian wig-type hairstyle, which may also here be associated with fertility. On some rectangular coffins, head-end panels are fashioned to simulate an Egyptian shrine, with cornice and supporting columns. The 'shrine' concept is taken further in some cupboard-type coffins with panels that can be opened to reveal the head and torso of the mummy within (figure 51), echoing that depicted in the Tomb of Petosiris at Tuna el-Gebel (figure 23).

Pottery coffins occur throughout the period, either plain or with the facial features sculpted on the lid, and have been found in areas of Greek/Roman

52. Slipper coffin (Roman Period). (Graeco-Roman Museum, Alexandria. Courtesy of Robert Partridge)

concentration – for example Taposiris Magna on the north coast, Bahariya Oasis and Kom Abu-Billou in the Delta. From Middle Egypt come body cases of dark red terracotta with geometric decoration and cursorily painted masks. A version of the pottery type is the 'slipper coffin' (figure 52), open at the head end for insertion of the corpse and sometimes decorated to simulate the rhomboidal mummy wrappings of the period.

Anthropoid coffins were used throughout the period (figure 53), often with nests of two or three inside massive outer coffins. At Saqqara during the early Ptolemaic Period shallow graves held roughly anthropoid coffins made of wooden planks dowelled together, plastered with thicker layers around the head and shoulders to enhance the mummiform effect, and subsequently painted to represent a mask and torso with *wesekh* collar. They reveal the social status of those who, not being able to afford an individual tomb, benefited from the nearby presence of the more ancient funerary complex. This concept of the body rather than the tomb being the focus after death became common practice in the Imperial Period. Characteristic of early Ptolemaic examples are large proportions, voluminous wigs, wide shoulders and high pedestal-type foot cases. Decoration consists of large *wesekh*-type collars sometimes extending over the whole torso, with winged figures of Nut and other funerary motifs, and panels of text on the back. Inner coffins are decorated with columns of funerary texts flanked by images of the four Sons of Horus, whose purpose it was to protect and revitalise the deceased. As the period progressed, an increase in fusion of Egyptian and Classical traditions can be observed, the registers of deities being relegated to the sides of the coffin and the deceased being represented in contemporary dress and hairstyle (figure 54).

53. Anthropoid wooden coffin of Horsanakht from Kharga Oasis (*c*.305 BC), with large *wesekh* collar on the breast with the goddess Nut below, a scene of the mummy on the funerary bier, protective deities and column of hieratic inscription. (Photograph by the author. British Museum: EA 52949)

Also during the Roman Period mummy boards, carved in relief, plastered and painted to give a mummiform and mask-like appearance, were often placed over the mummy within the coffin and separate boards with funerary texts were also often inserted.

Cartonnage body cases

The focus of emphasis in the Graeco-Roman Period tended to be on the body and its accoutrements rather than on the tomb in which it was placed and, although standards in mummification declined, the outer coverings were often very elaborate. Cartonnage was manufactured by fusing layers of

54. Wooden coffin, from Middle Egypt, of a girl dressed in contemporary tunic and mantle, wearing snake bracelets and a floral wreath and holding a sprig of myrtle. The sides are decorated with scenes of Egyptian iconography (mid first century AD). (British Museum: EA 29587. Graphics courtesy of Derek Edwards)

55. Anthropoid mummy case of Djedhor from Akhmim (*c.*250 BC), wrapped and coated in black resin and supporting a gilded mask and separate cartonnage plaques decorated with *wesekh* collar, the goddess Nut and the four Sons of Horus. (Photograph by the author. British Museum: EA 29776)

linen or papyrus together with glue and gesso to form separate appliqués, masks, body plaques, foot cases and complete anthropoid mummy cases, elaborately and brightly painted with images of Osiris, the sun-god Ra, the Sons of Horus and scenes of the deceased on his bier and being purified by lustration, all taken from Egyptian funerary iconography. However, the influence of the ruling culture gradually became apparent with the emergence of a mixed style incorporating Egyptian elements with more naturalistic rendering of the facial features. The transition can be seen in a series dating to the first century BC from Akhmim (figure 55). Early in the series, separate pieces of cartonnage are placed over the mummy, to include a gilded face mask, with large painted eyes and voluminous wig, a pectoral incorporating a *wesekh* collar with complex floral motifs and representations of Nut and the Sons of Horus,

and a long plaque or separate appliqués covering the lower abdomen and legs, similarly decorated with either another *wesekh*-style collar or scenes of the mummy on the bier, amuletic *djed* symbols, the Sons of Horus and jackals guarding the door to Hades. The feet also have a separate covering, often modelled in relief, figuratively to enable the deceased to walk in the afterlife.

Towards the end of the Ptolemaic Period the mask is similarly gilded but the eyes are now encrusted and the traditional wig is replaced by a winged solar disk with diadem and band of uraei on the brow and depictions of Egyptian gods on the back. The *wesekh* collar now forms part of the mask rather than a separate pectoral. The body case is decorated as in the earlier group and the foot case bears relief stucco, sometimes gilded, shaped to represent feet wearing strapped sandals. Both these groups are decorated in the strong, dark colours of the Ptolemaic Period – dark reds, blues and greens with beiges, yellow and gilding. From the late Ptolemaic into the Imperial Period there is a change in colour palette to much use of pink, green, yellow, cream and gold (figure 56). Body cases are mummiform

56. Anthropoid mummy case of a man, made of cartonnage, canvas and stucco painted to represent network, from Akhmim (late first century BC); pectoral with geometric motifs, and scenes from Egyptian funerary iconography on lower body; face individualistically painted in light flesh tones with black beard. (Photograph by the author. British Museum: EA 29584)

57. Anthropoid mummy case of Taminis, from Akhmim (late first century BC), painted and gilded, represented as if wearing contemporary dress closely adhering to the shape of the body; the face is gilded and the image wears a striped head-dress with pink floral wreath and diadem. (Photograph by the author. British Museum: EA 29586)

with wide shoulders giving a hunched effect and sometimes with the arms revealed. The face, which is often gilded, is enveloped by a large winged solar disk with uraei. On the breast the use of the *wesekh* collar is now discontinued in favour of more simple collars with geometric motifs. The body is encased in simulated network emulating the bead-net coverings of the Late Period, traditionally representing the wrappings of Osiris and, by association, rebirth. The lower body is adorned with representations of the goddess Nut, Horus and the mummy on the bier, each separated by panels of geometric motifs. The last scene is usually of Anubis as a black jackal guarding the mummy flanked by two falcons. The feet again wear strapped sandals.

Of similar date is a group of body cases where the traditional Egyptian mummy form has been modified to follow the shape of the body, and the deceased is portrayed in contemporary dress with the arms down by the side or holding the mantle to the body (figure 57). Now, for the first time in the series, the deceased is shown with his/her own hair, sometimes composed of vegetable fibres, beneath a wreath of flowers. The eyes are large, emphasising divine status. Faces are sometimes gilded, but most have light-coloured flesh. On female figures fecundity is represented by prominent breasts, gilded or emphasised by floral motifs, and by revealing the shape of the body, even down to an indication of the navel and pubic area, beneath the tight drapery. They are also bedecked with jewellery in the style of the late first century BC to early first century AD. Feet are encased in strapped sandals.

5
Masks and portraits

Cartonnage masks

Cartonnage masks were also manufactured as separate headpieces for mummies encased in canvas, cartonnage, plaster and linen. In the Ptolemaic Period casque-shaped helmets enveloping the entire head became fashionable (figure 58). The design and decoration follow Egyptian tradition, but signs of Greek influence became more apparent as the period progressed, with more naturalistic faces, fleshy cheeks and chins, smiling mouths and large ears positioned high on the head.

Regional diversity is also apparent. From Meir comes a series of canvas and stucco masks fitted over the head

58. (Left) Painted cartonnage funerary mask from Sedment (Ptolemaic Period). (Bolton Museum: 1910.54.21. Copyright of the Trustees of Bolton Museum)

59. (Below) Mummy of Anoubias (mid first century AD), wrapped in thick padding, with high feet, and the head and bust covered with a mask similar to that in figure 60. The sides hold appliqués of stuccoed canvas, painted and gilded to represent Anubis, Osiris, Isis, Horus and Sokar. (Museum of Egyptian Antiquities: 33137. After Edgar)

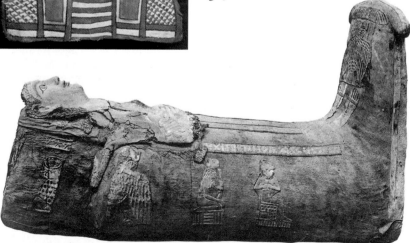

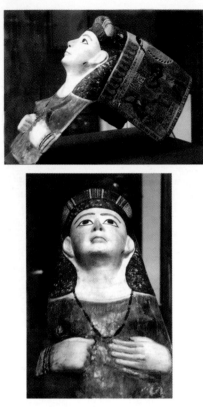

60. Painted canvas and stucco funerary mask of a woman, from Meir (mid first century AD), dressed in a chiton and wearing a necklace, bracelets and earrings and a rolled head wreath with geometric designs. On the back are a central figure of Osiris and a human-headed winged hawk, flanked on the right by Horus making offering to Osiris and on the left by Anubis offering to Sokar. (Museum of Egyptian Antiquities, Cairo: 33130. Graphics courtesy of Derek Edwards)

ends of mummies thickly padded out to take the shape of a high-footed anthropoid coffin (figure 59). The facial features are modelled in a combination of Greek naturalistic and Egyptian stylistic features (figure 60). The flesh is cream with pink lines to accentuate folds of flesh, and the lips and nostrils are painted red. Eyes are inlaid with white glass or limestone, surrounded by a blue glass strip, elongated at the outer edges in the Egyptian style. The hair is modelled from vegetable fibre and subsequently painted, and the image wears a rolled head-dress with geometric motifs or a wreath of separately made petals, symbolising a botanical funerary crown. The dress is contemporary – a tunic and sometimes an overmantle which envelops the right arm. On some female masks naked breasts are moulded in plaster, painted naturalistically in pink or gilded, again as symbols of fertility in the afterlife (figure 61). The mask is extended to wrap around the head end of the coffin and is covered with scenes of Egyptian mythology and funerary iconography

61. Painted cartonnage mask and bust of a woman (*c.*AD 100) dressed in contemporary clothes but also wearing an Egyptian-style pectoral with winged scarab. The breasts are exposed to indicate fertility. Provenance unknown, but probably from Middle Egypt. (British Museum: EA 29476. Courtesy of Robert Partridge)

– deities adoring and offering to Osiris or other gods, bordered by friezes of Greek metopes and stars – and on the crown either a winged scarab, a hawk, a vulture, a *djed* pillar or an Osiris figure flanked by jackals.

Gilded masks

Gold was believed to protect the body from degeneration and symbolise the newly acquired divinity of the deceased, and a series of gilded masks also reveals the beginnings of more individualistic portrait features (figure 62). Heavy moulded gilding covers the face and, on richer examples, the whole of the head. Eyes are

62. Painted and gilded cartonnage mask from the Fayum (first century AD). (Bolton Museum: 1902.53.20. Copyright of the Trustees of Bolton Museum)

63. (Left) Gilded cartonnage mask (first century AD) from Tomb 54, Bahariya Oasis. The hair is modelled in tight curls with Greek-style diadem and Egyptian uraeus. The face has distinctly individualistic features despite the Egyptian manner in which the eyes are rendered. (El-Bawiti Museum, Bahariya Oasis. Courtesy of Robert Partridge)

64. (Below) Gilded mask incorporating head, shoulders, bust and arms, *in situ* on a painted cartonnage mummy of a girl (mid first century AD). She is dressed in a tunic with *clavi*, mantle drawn over the head and shoulders and heavy gold jewellery, and she holds a folded garland of rose petals. Her hair is waved, with centre parting, curls and ringlets. Her eyes are inlaid, her mouth is set in a smile and her chin dimpled. (Courtesy of The Manchester Museum)

often inlaid with painted glass and semi-precious stones and the head is enveloped in a gilded winged sun-disk. The shoulders, back and lappets are decorated with scenes from Egyptian funerary iconography – the deceased on the bier attended by Anubis, and representations of deities and funerary symbols: *Ba*-birds, jackals, sphinxes and winged cobras. There is also an interesting use of the uraeus and the vulture, formerly the prerogative of Egyptian royalty (figure 63), and now appropriated for non-royal personages. The richness of decoration implies that, in life, these people would have been of a high social status. Dating from the late first century BC to the early second century AD, inscriptions give names of the individuals and other personal data such as affiliation. On later examples the subject is portrayed in the clothes of daily life, men being dressed in a Roman tunic with *clavi*, and women in tunics and mantles drawn over the head and bedecked with jewellery, but retaining the Egyptian iconographical scenes on the back of the mask and body covering (figure 64).

65. Modelled and painted bust of a man; stuccoed canvas mounted on a linen base (*c.*AD 220–50). The flesh is painted naturalistically in shades of pink and the hair is black and curly. He wears a white tunic, large winged pendant and wreath of white leaves and red berries. He holds a cup and folded garland. Beneath the bust is a zone of ornamental motifs and a mythological scene of the barque of Sokar flanked by jackals. (Museum of Egyptian Antiquities, Cairo: 33277. After Edgar)

Masks attached to linen

Late in the period a series of modelled plaster portraits attached to linen shrouds comes from Deir el-Bahri, dated by style and hairstyle to *c.*AD 220–50 (figure 65). Reaching to almost a metre in length, they comprise a three-dimensional bust of the deceased portrayed frontally in the manner of late Roman funerary portraiture. Predominant colours are pink hues for the flesh, cream and yellows for the dress, with browns, purples and olive greens. All wear long-sleeved tunics with *clavi*, mantles, heavy gold jewellery and floral diadem. In one hand the image holds a cup of wine, which may be the equivalent in portraiture of representing the importance of the vine in funerary iconography, as seen on sarcophagi, biers and tomb walls and symbolic of fruitfulness, and in the other hand a folded floral garland. Below a border of floral motifs is a scene showing the barque of the Memphite funerary god, Sokar, flanked by jackals as guides of the deceased and guardians of the entrance to the underworld (Hades).

Plaster heads

A series of plaster heads dates from the early first century to the middle of the third century AD (figure 66). Provenance has, in many instances, been poorly recorded, but the type seems to have been prevalent in Middle Egypt and many originate from Tuna el-Gebel. Manufactured to be placed over the head ends of flat wooden coffins, the heads, when complete, would have incorporated shoulders and breast, but many have been broken away from their original emplacements. Made from moulds, the heads have been painted naturalistically, following Classical tradition, which gives them their individualistic appearance. They can be dated by hairstyles, analysis of the clothing, which is of the day – tunics, mantles and jewellery, and by a certain

66. Plaster head of a woman. The hair is waved close to the head into a bun at the back. The eyebrows and lashes are indicated by cross-hatching and the eyes are inlaid glass. The jewellery and hairstyle date the piece to the Antonine Period. (Courtesy of The Manchester Museum: 11250)

stylistic development. The earlier examples are not dissimilar to the masks from Meir but the heads are slightly raised at an angle. Eyes are mostly painted on but a few are inlaid with opaque stone or glass. On many of the female masks of this type the hair is in the Egyptian style with side tresses, while the male coiffure is short and combed forward in the style popular in Rome during the first half of the first century AD.

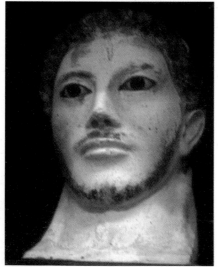

67. Plaster head of a man with naturalistic features and facial hair (mid second century AD). (Graeco-Roman Museum, Alexandria)

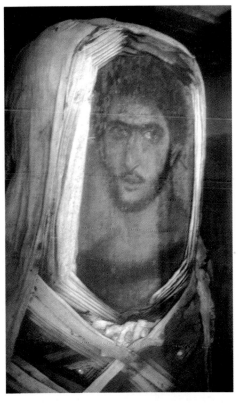

68. Portrait in wrappings (mid second century AD). (Museum of Egyptian Antiquities, Cairo: 33243. Courtesy of Robert Partridge)

Many wear wreaths simulating rose petals. The head rises gradually throughout the period until the later examples appear as if propped up by a high pillow and are more naturalistic in form (figure 67), more divorced from Egyptian constraints, and the painted eyes are now overlain by a thin layer of glass.

Painted portraits

At the beginning of the first century AD the practice of placing a flat-painted portrait on the mummy came into use and this continued up to the end of the third century AD. Found mainly in places where a high concentration of Greeks and Romans settled, such as the Fayum towns and Antinoopolis, these images represent the deceased as a two-dimensional head and shoulders portrait painted on flat wooden boards or on linen. Their style is totally Classical and they appear incongruous wrapped in elaborate rhomboidal mummy bindings or encased in cartonnage in the Egyptian tradition (figure 68). Two painting techniques have been used: encaustic, the pigments being mixed with wax or resin and applied, either hot or cold, with a brush, *cauterium* or *cestrum*; and tempera, using brushes of palm fibre or natural hair. Pigments used were made from natural ochres, animal and vegetable dyes and applied over a layer of gesso. The use of different depths of colour, shading and highlighting creates a lifelike appearance which is enhanced by the manner in which the subject is depicted in perspectival three-quarter pose with the shoulders slightly turned and the head inclined to face the viewer, as if caught in a moment of time. Dating is established by analysis of hairstyles, clothes and jewellery, which follow the fashions of Imperial Rome and also indicate the wealth, status and area of domicile of the deceased (figure 69). Some are inscribed with names, such as

Eirene, Hermione, Artemidorus and Eutyches, and many complete examples were accompanied by labels giving the name, profession, place of origin and destination of the mummy. Some of the men are shown naked, which may indicate their gymnasium affiliation or heroisation after death, because in Greek iconography the soul mingled in the afterlife with the heroes of old. Religious belief is sometimes indicated, for example a male wearing a star diadem demonstrating affiliation to the cult of Serapis. Likewise, women wearing knotted shawls and curls around the face may be adherents of the cult of Isis. Profession is not so easy to identify, but some men wear a cloak and *balteus* indicating that they were soldiers.

The individualistic appearance of the portraits, in contrast to the Egyptian treatment of the body to which they are attached, has led to the suggestion that they may have been painted from life and re-used

70. Portrait of a man in tempera on a wooden panel (*c.*AD 110–30); from Er-Rubayat. (British Museum: EA 63397. Courtesy of Dr Peter Dixon)

after death. That framed portraits existed is confirmed by the discovery of one such example found lying against a mummy without an integral portrait, and, indeed, most boards were originally rectangular and have been subsequently trimmed. However, the majority of the subjects are portrayed in the prime of life, and while some radiological studies (CAT scans) carried out on mummies with portraits intact do confirm a relationship between the mortal remains and the portrait, others have revealed discrepancies of age and gender. Facial reconstructions have also been made, some of which do resemble the portraits, and it is entirely plausible that some of the more accomplished examples were painted from life. However, when looking at the corpus of portraits as a whole, various groupings can be discerned, based on resemblances of physiognomy and racial types. Moreover, different hands and workshops with their own particular styles can be distinguished and stylistic development can be traced from the individualistic early portraits to the linear and abstract examples towards the end of the period.

Many of the portraits may have been carried in the *ekphora*, as described by Pliny, then placed on the mummy in a shrine-type coffin and displayed in a domestic context or above-ground pavilion as at Marina el-Alamein, giving weight to the theory that they were kept above ground, before being discarded in communal graves. Overall, the portraits represent the social standing of the deceased within their own local communities, as descendants of the original Greek colonists, landowners, administrators, ex-military personnel – a local elite striving to demonstrate their allegiance to Rome.

71. Portrait of a young boy on a linen shroud, holding a myrtle branch and raising his right hand, and dressed in tunic, mantle and wreath. His coffin lid is decorated with a snake and the interior of the base holds the image of the goddess Nut. (Photograph by the author. British Museum: EA 6715)

Painted shrouds

Thickly padded mummies have already been mentioned in relation to the masks from Meir. These were wrapped in resin-soaked linen, bulked out to resemble coffins and decorated with painted stucco appliqués of divinities. Throughout the period the body itself was sometimes directly adorned: during the Ptolemaic Period the eyelids and lips, fingers and toes and genital areas were sometimes gilded, and in the Roman Period gold plates were placed on the eyes, lips and tongue before the body was carefully wrapped in three-dimensional rhomboidal formation bandages, sometimes with a gold stud in the centre of each lozenge. Also at this time, some mummies were wrapped in stiffened linen shrouds painted red to emulate cartonnage, with the facial features, clothing and funerary scenes cursorily indicated on the cloth, or with a painted portrait incorporated.

Running in parallel to the panel portraits is a series of shrouds with the facial features painted in tempera directly on to the linen (figure 71). The technique is similar to that of the linen-based portraits and dating is based on the same criteria, but there is regional variety of style. On the shrouds of the Soter burials from Thebes, male figures are represented as if enveloped in the bead net of Osiris whereas the women are shown frontally in the style of the figures of Nut on the interior of their coffins. On some shrouds from Antinoopolis the deceased is portrayed full-length, dressed in contemporary clothing, with the weight transferred on to the left leg in the Greek artistic tradition, and some later examples are depicted frontally, following Roman trends, but at the same time the adherence to Egyptian funerary beliefs is demonstrated by the presence of Egyptian gods, Osiris, Anubis and Sokar. On a painted shroud from Saqqara the portrait has been executed separately and inserted into the rest of the shroud. This may be evidence of a funerary industry preparing 'off-the-shelf' shrouds and portraits ready to be personalised.

6
Cinerary urns

Cremation was practised in Alexandria during the Ptolemaic Period and excavations in the city and its environs have revealed a series of cinerary urns, predominantly hydriae and some amphorae, dating from the beginning of the Ptolemaic Period up to *c.*200 BC. Find sites include pit graves, niches and loculi. Decorative motifs – floral, garland, linear and geometric designs and some animal figures – closely follow those of West Slope ware, which was prevalent throughout the Eastern Mediterranean in the Hellenistic period. There are, however, adaptations in the style unique to the Alexandrian series. Several classes occur.

Black-ground class (figure 72)

This group is identified by black glaze, vertical ribbing, stylised garland decoration in red, white and yellow pigments mixed with thinned clay, applied with a thin brush, and the use of incision. Motifs used are sprays of ivy or vine leaves, egg-and-dart motifs interspersed with dots, rosettes and stars. As the series progressed, the designs became more elaborate, the decoration extending over the body and incorporating geometric and wave patterns. Some have appliqué designs of Medusa heads and larger female figures and the inspiration for this class may have been metal receptacles. Remains of painted stucco indicate that some may also have been gilded, perhaps imitating designs on Alexandrian gold glass vessels.

White-ground class (figure 73)

In this group, the vessel has been coated, after firing, with a thin coat of white calcium carbonate as a background for polychrome decoration. Analysis of the clay points to an Alexandrian origin; it is coarse-grained and of a light reddish hue, porous and highly impractical for anything other than funerary use. As the decoration was added after firing, few

72. Black-ground amphora with polychrome decoration (third century BC); Necropolis of Shatby, Alexandria.

73. White-ground hydria with separate neck garland (third century BC); Necropolis of Shatby.

urns have retained much of their original paint, impeding attempts to trace stylistic development or dating, but most were discovered in the oldest parts of the Necropolis of Shatby (*c.*325 to *c.*240 BC). Decoration again takes the form of garland and floral motifs but now in a wide variety of colours – blue, green, red, brown and yellow – freely applied in an informal style directly on to the white ground of the vessel (figure 74). A variety of hues is used in an attempt to represent the natural plant colours and sometimes a separate garland of terracotta or faience leaves and flowers was also hung around the neck of the vessel. Pictorial designs occur – grave

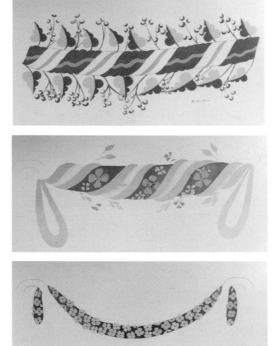

74. Reproduction of floral garland motifs on white-ground hydriae from the Necropolis of Shatby, Alexandria. (After Breccia)

monuments and stelae painted yellow and red, representations in miniature of actual grave markers. Personal possessions and equipment are also featured, particularly military equipment for the men and mirrors and toilet boxes for the women.

Clay-ground class (figure 75)

This is the largest group, consisting of more than three hundred specimens. Commonly termed 'Hadra vases', after the cemetery in which many of them were found, the class consists of clay-ground vessels decorated, before firing, in predominantly black or brown with some added colour to pick out detail. Analysis of the clay has indicated a Cretan manufacture for certain groups of this class but their use predominantly in Alexandria indicates a specific market. The class is particularly important for dating purposes, many being inscribed with the names of the deceased and the undertaker, the date of the funeral and the year and name of the reigning monarch. However, all the kings of the dynasty were named Ptolemy, which complicates matters, but a detailed stylistic analysis places them from the mid third to the early second century BC, with time spans for individual sub-groups based on characteristics of form and decoration pinned around those examples that can be securely dated. At first glance the decoration seems uniform, but various workshops, hands and styles can be observed. The motifs used also closely follow those of West Slope ware but in the reverse

75. Clay-ground Hadra hydria with dolphin decoration; Necropolis of Hadra.

colour scheme – dark on light. Garland decoration predominates, ranging from simple wreaths of leaves to more complex sprays of ivy, interspersed with dot rosettes, linear and geometric motifs, and the palmette is commonly used for the back of the vessel. Animal themes also occur, particularly lively scenes of winged horses and plunging dolphins, enhanced by the use of incision and applied colour. In Greek funerary iconography, these were the creatures which carried the soul of the deceased to the afterworld, confirming that these vessels were designed for funerary use. Scenes of hunting and combat also occur, and some athletic pursuits. Inscriptions reveal that they contained the cremated remains of diplomats and military personnel on official service in the city. The series does not continue into the Roman Period, when inhumation, rather than cremation, became the standard practice in the Eastern Roman Empire.

7
The art-historical legacy

The Alexandrian hypogea derive from Macedonian prototypes, but innovation in plan and decoration indicates the freedom of the immigrants to develop their own style, while still maintaining links to their native cultures. The value of the architectonic decoration here is that it pre-dates similar features in Style I from Pompeii, and its development can be traced from the simple work at Shatby, through the zone-style at Mustapha Kamel, to the full-blown masonry style and its degeneration at Anfushy, and its elaboration at Antinoopolis and Tuna el-Gebel. Innovation can also be seen in the peristyle architectural forms of Shatby, Mustapha Kamel and the portals of Anfushy, all used to enhance the illusion of receding space. Likewise, the concept of optical illusion to 'open up' the wall pre-dates the Pompeian Style II.

The impressionistic manner of the Painted Tomb from Wardiyan likens the painting to Pompeian Style III and, if a late Ptolemaic date is assigned to the tomb, then this is a very important precursor to the style. The Mustapha Kamel frieze and the funerary stelae from Alexandria play an important role in the history of Greek figure painting. The tendency for Egyptianising decoration appears in the later Ptolemaic Period in the Anfushy and Ras el-Tin necropoleis but it is not until the Roman Period that a true mix of styles occurs, seen particularly in the Kom el-Shugafa complex and the Tigrane Tomb. This mixed style has often been called 'degenerate' because the former significance of particularly the Egyptian motifs has been forgotten. It is nevertheless important evidence of inter-cultural influence and may better be termed 'art in transition'.

In contrast to Egyptianising tendencies in the capital, we can see the hellenising of Egyptian burial customs in the provinces. Burial customs, in general, are heavily influenced by religion and in this field it was the policy of the new order to encourage and promote local practices. The process of religious mutation can be seen in varying degrees in the material studied. The mixed styles in the tomb of Petosiris of Tuna el-Gebel, for example, are an indication of the duality of approach the priesthood would have adopted. In the tombs of the oases and Upper Egypt the decoration follows Egyptian tradition, but with the stamping of Greek influence – for example, in the manner in which Petosiris of Dakhleh demonstrates his allegiance to Rome in his dress and in the way provincial stelae from the seats of religious importance and nome capitals portray more Greek influence. The powerful tradition of the Egyptian gods and the spectacular burial customs of Ancient Egypt must have appeared very attractive to the immigrants and mummification was retained throughout the Graeco-Roman period. The hellenising of the process can be observed in the coffins and mummy cases from Akhmim. The tendency to individualise can be seen in the masks, plaster heads and mummy cases but the extent to which they are hellenised varies, the high-status gilded examples appearing less so than those of decorated cartonnage, the latter perhaps belonging to a middle class aspiring to a higher social status by appearing to be more hellenised.

A similar theory may apply to the portrait mummies. Funerary portraiture has a long history in Roman commemorative sculpture, but never in such close contact with the human remains as in Egypt, and this may contribute to the individualistic nature of the painted portraits. It is nevertheless entirely plausible that some of the most accomplished portraits were painted during the lifetime of the subject and that, once the custom of re-using them after death had taken root, a funerary industry became established. On all of them, the eyes are unusually large and expressive. The eyes are the feature that brings a portrait to life, which is the purpose of the mummy, and in this respect their subjects have indeed achieved 'immortality'. They are of incalculable importance to the history of painted portraiture and are the most dramatic result of the meeting of three great cultures – Egyptian mummification and funerary iconography, Greek technical achievements and Roman veristic portraiture. The degree of hellenisation in all the categories is evidence of how the nome capitals, seats of religious importance and areas of high concentrations of Greek and Roman settlement had become influenced by the incoming culture, but at the same time they indicate the tolerance, encouragement and adoption of local burial customs by the immigrant population and their descendants.

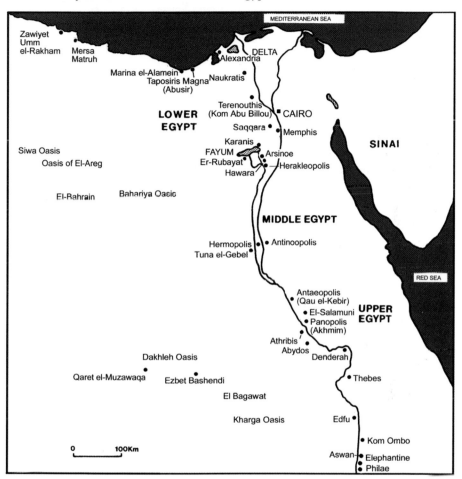

76. Map of Egypt showing sites of the Graeco-Roman period.

8
Glossary

Acroterion (plural **acroteria**): ornamental device on the corners and gable ends of roofs and pediments.

Aedicula: a small shrine or niche with columns supporting a pediment.

Aesclepius: the Greek god of healing, often accompanied by the image of a snake, which, emerging from the ground, represents healing and rebirth.

Agathodaemon: literally 'good spirit'; a benevolent snake god.

Amun: the main god of Thebes and head of the Egyptian pantheon. His oracle was at Siwa.

Antefix: ornamental device on the side of a roof.

Anthropoid: human form.

Anubis: Egyptian jackal-headed god of the dead, responsible for mummification and protection of the tomb; often represented as a black jackal.

Aphrodite: Greek goddess of love.

Apis: sacred bull of the Egyptians, associated with the god Ptah of Memphis and symbolising strength and fertility.

Apotheosis: deification or glorification.

Apse: a semicircular or polygonal recess.

Architectonic: painted decoration simulating courses of masonry or stone revetments and architectural elements.

Arcosolium (plural *arcosolia*): an arched alcove.

Ashlar: rectangular saw-cut blocks of stone laid in regular courses.

Atef **crown**: the crown of the sun-god Ra and Osiris in Egyptian iconography.

Ba-**bird**: spirit of the deceased equating to the personality, represented by a human-headed bird.

Balteus: sword strap worn over the shoulder.

Barque: boat.

Barrel vault: a vault with a simple hemicylindrical roof.

Bucranium (plural *bucrania*): ox skull used as a sacrificial symbol to decorate temples, altars and funerary contexts.

Caduceus: the wand of Hermes, consisting of a staff with entwined snakes and two small wings on the top.

Canopic jars: four vessels containing the preserved internal organs of the deceased.

Cartonnage: layers of linen or papyrus fused together with glue and gesso.

CAT: Computerised Axial Tomography.

Cauterium: a burning iron.

Cestrum: pointed instrument used for engraving.

Chiton: a Greek tunic.

Chlamys: a short Greek cloak.

Classical: period in Greek history from the fifth to the fourth century BC.

Clavus (plural *clavi*): one of the stripes on a Roman tunic indicating rank and status.

Demotic: a simplified form of handwritten hieroglyphs, the everyday script of the Graeco-Roman Period.

Dexiosis: the clasping of the right hands in greeting or farewell.

Dionysus: Greek god of wine and revelry, associated with fruitfulness and rebirth.

Djed **pillar**: amulet representing the backbone of Osiris.

Doric: one of the Greek orders of architecture, comprising fluted columns without bases and with cushion capitals, supporting a frieze of metopes and triglyphs.

Dromos (plural **dromoi**): rock-cut, open-air, sloping access way to a tomb.

Ekphora: the funeral procession.

Encaustic: a method of painting using melted wax.

Eros (plural *erotes*): cupid.

Fresco: method of applying paint to wet plaster.

Gesso: a plaster surface prepared as a ground for painting.

Gouache: a method of watercolour painting with opaque colours mixed with water or gum.

Hades: the Greek god of the underworld, also meaning the underworld itself; the place where souls go after death.

Harpocrates: the Greek form of the Egyptian god Horus the Child, son of Isis and Osiris.

Hellenistic: Greek historical period, third to first century BC.

Hermanubis: form of Anubis combined with Hermes as a soldier god, guardian of the dead and conqueror of the enemies of the dead.

Hermes: a Greek god, the messenger of the gods.

Hermes Psychopompos: the Greek god who accompanies the dead to the afterlife.

Himation: Greek form of overmantle or cloak.

Horus: Egyptian god of the sky, son of Isis and Osiris, represented by a falcon.

Hydria (plural **hydriae**): a large Greek water vase with two horizontal handles at the shoulder and a vertical handle at the back.

Hypogeum (plural **hypogea**): an underground tomb, usually comprising several chambers.

Inhumation: burial or interment of human remains.

Intarsia: inlay work.

Ionic: Greek order of architecture with fluted columns on bases, scroll-shaped capitals and frieze of egg-and-dart motifs.

Isis: Egyptian goddess, the sister and wife of Osiris and mother of Horus; in the Graeco-Roman period, the wife of Serapis.

Isis-Sothis: assimilation of the astral goddess Sothis into Isis, personifying fecundity and rebirth.

Ka: in Egyptian funerary iconography, the soul or life-force of a person.

Kline (plural *klinai*): couch.

Lappet: part of a wig or head-dress framing the face and neck and extending to the shoulders.

Lenos: bench-type sarcophagus.

Loculus (plural **loculi**): a rock-cut cavity used for burials.

Lotiform: shaped in the form of the Egyptian lotus flower.

Lunette: space formed at the top of walls below a vaulted ceiling.

Lustration: purification by sacrifice or washing.

Maenad: a Greek wood-nymph.

Mastaba: ancient Egyptian tomb shaped in the form of a bench.

Medusa: Greek mythological creature with the head of a woman and hair of snakes, who turned to stone all those who gazed upon her.

Metope: the slabs of a Doric frieze.

Nabataean: style similar to 'Nabataean' architecture at Petra, Jordan, and now thought to derive from Graeco-Roman Egypt.

Naos: the inner and most important chamber or shrine of a temple or tomb.

Necropolis (plural **necropoleis**): cemetery.

Nemesis: the Greek goddess of retribution and justice.

Nephthys: Egyptian funerary goddess, the sister of Osiris.

Nike (plural *nikai*): winged goddess of victory.

Nome: administrative region of Egypt.

Nut: Egyptian sky-goddess, mother of Osiris, Isis and Nephthys.

Oculus: circular aperture, usually in a domed ceiling.

Oikos: literally meaning 'chamber'; here intended to mean the form of tomb with chambers in linear formation.

Orans: the raising of arms in an attitude of prayer or adoration.

Osiris: Egyptian god of funerary protection, fertility and rebirth.

Ourobouros: double-headed snake-like creature, symbol of eternal life.

Papyriform: shaped like the papyrus plant.

Pectoral: ornament worn on the breast.

Pediment: triangular structure crowning the front of a Greek building or over a door or window.

Peristyle: pillared colonnade in Greek architecture.

Persephone: Greek goddess abducted by Hades and who returned to spend half the year in the land of the living and the remainder in Hades.

Pharos: the ancient lighthouse at Alexandria; one of the seven wonders of the world.

Pilaster: square-shaped pillar attached to a wall.

Polychrome: the art of decorating in many colours.

Pompeian: styles of decoration in Pompeii: Style I, *c.*150–90 BC; Style II, *c.*90–20 BC; Style III, *c.*20 BC–AD 62; Style IV, AD 62–79.

Portico: range of columns along the front or side of a building or courtyard.

Pronaos: antechamber to main sanctuary.

Prothesis: the laying out of the deceased prior to interment.

Ra: the Egyptian creator sun-god.

Rotunda: circular chamber.

Sacral-idyllic: literally meaning 'consecrated-sacred place', a work of art portraying the simplicity of a rustic setting.

Saqqiyeh: a water-raising device, operated by beasts of burden.

Sarcophagus: literally meaning 'body eater', a large container for burials.

Satyr: Greek wood-god with tail and long ears, sometimes represented as a goat or as a being composed of part man, part lion, part antelope.

Scarab: the Egyptian dung-beetle.

Secco: method of applying paint to dry plaster.

Serapis: a new god in Egypt created by Ptolemy I to incorporate the powers of the Egyptian gods Osiris and Apis and the Greek gods Zeus, Helios, Dionysus and Aesclepius. Represented as a bearded man wearing a corn measure. God of healing, wisdom and fruitfulness.

Sokar: Egyptian hawk-god of the dead and of the Memphite necropolis.

Sons of Horus: guardians of the organs of the deceased inside the Canopic jars.

Sphinx: figure with the body of a lion and the face of a human or another animal.

Stela (plural **stelae**): stone slab, here a gravestone or marker.

Stucco: plaster used for coating walls prior to decoration.

Tempera: a method of painting with pigments mixed with water and gum.

Tessera (plural **tesserae**): mosaic cube.

Thoth: Egyptian God of wisdom and knowledge; the scribe of the gods, represented as either an ibis or baboon.

Thyrsus: the wand carried by Dionysus; a staff topped by a pine-cone and/or ivy or vine leaves.

Triclinium: a Roman dining-room with couches on three sides.

Triglyph: slab with three vertical grooves in a Doric frieze.

Trompe l'oeil: literally meaning 'deceipt of the eye'; the simulation in paint of three-dimensional objects as if seen in perspective on a two-dimensional surface.

Tympanum: the recessed face of a pediment.

Uraeus (plural **uraei**): the image of the Egyptian hooded cobra, symbol of kingship in Ancient Egypt, adopted and used in a protective capacity in the Graeco-Roman Period.

Verism: truth-like. A manner of representation in Roman sculpture and painting, seeking to render a realistic image of the protagonist.

Wadjet: Egyptian cobra goddess.

Wesekh: Egyptian collar with falcon-headed terminals and bands of floral decoration placed over the breasts of mummies to invoke protection and fecundity.

West Slope ware: a class of Greek vases with light-on-dark geometric and garland decoration, named for its find site on the west slope of the Acropolis; Hellenistic Period.

Zeus: the greatest of the Greek gods, identified in Egypt with Amun.

Zone-style: a scheme of painted decoration arranged in zones or layers differentiated by colour.

9
Further reading

Books on the burial customs of Ancient Egypt in general have sections covering the Graeco-Roman Period, but there is no definitive work comprising all the categories for all of the periods covered in this book. Some of the categories have been published in depth, particularly works on the painted portraits and masks, but others, such as some of the rock-cut tombs of Upper Egypt and the oases and, particularly, the cinerary urns, can be found only in academic journals and excavation reports – hence their inclusion here.

Historical and general background
Bowman, A. K. *Egypt after the Pharaohs.* British Museum Press, London, 1986.
Ellis, S. P. *Graeco-Roman Egypt.* Shire, Princes Risborough, 1992.
Empereur, J-Y. *The Graeco-Roman Museum, Alexandria.* Sarapis Publishing, Alexandria, 1995.
Empereur, J-Y. *Alexandria Rediscovered.* British Museum Press, London, 1998. Includes a section on the most recent excavations in the necropoleis of Gabbari and Plinthine.

Burial customs
Dodson, A., and Ikram, S. *The Mummy in Ancient Egypt.* Thames & Hudson, London, 1998.
Grajetzki, W. *Burial Customs in Ancient Egypt.* Duckworth, London, 2003.
Riggs, C. *The Beautiful Burial in Roman Egypt.* Oxford University Press, Oxford, 2006.
Spencer, A. J. *Death in Ancient Egypt.* Penguin Books, London, 1982; reprinted 1991.

Rock-cut tombs
Daszewski, W. A. 'Excavations at Marina el-Alamein', in *Mitteilungen des Deutschen Archäologischen Instituts Abteilung Kairo*, 46, 15–51; Cairo, 1990.
Dunand, F.; Heim, J-L.; Henein, N.; and Lichtenberg, R. *La Nécropole de Douch (Oasis de Kharga).* Institut Français d'Archéologie Orientale, Cairo, 1992.
El-Farag, R.; Kaplony-Heckel, U.; and Kuhlmann, K. P. 'Athribis', in *Mitteilungen des Deutschen Archäologischen Instituts Abteilung Kairo*, 41; Cairo, 1985.
Empereur, J-Y. *The Catacombs of Kom el-Shugafa.* Sarapis Publishing, Alexandria, 1995.
Empereur, J-Y. *Necropolis 1.* Institut Français d'Archéologie Orientale, Cairo, 2001. Excavation reports on the Necropolis of Gabbari, Alexandria.
Fakhry, A. *The Necropolis of El-Bagawat in Kharga Oasis.* Service des Antiquités de l'Égypte, Cairo, 1951.
Fakhry, A. *Siwa Oasis.* American University in Cairo Press, Cairo, 1973; reprinted 1990. Includes a description of the tombs of Gebel Mawta.
Gabra, S. *Peintures à Fresques et Scènes Peintes à Hermoupolis-Ouest (Touna el-Gebel).* Service des Antiquités de l'Égypte, Cairo, 1954.
Lefebvre, G. *Le Tombeau de Petosiris.* Service des Antiquités de l'Égypte, Cairo, 1924.
Osing, J.; Moursi, M.; Arnold, D.; Neugebauer, O.; Parker, R. A.; Pingree, D.; and Nur-el-Din, M. A. *Denkmaler der Oase Dachla.* Deutsches Archäologisches Institut,

Cairo, 1982. Includes a description of the tombs at Ezbet Bashendi and Qaret el-Muzawaqa.

Petrie, Sir W. M. F. *Athribis.* British School of Archaeology in Egypt, London, 1908.

Venit, M. S. *Monumental Tombs of Ancient Alexandria.* Cambridge University Press, Cambridge, 2002. Includes a resumé of previous excavation reports.

Voros, G. *Taposiris Magna.* Egypt Excavation Society of Hungary, Budapest, 2001.

Loculus slabs and funerary stelae

Abdalla, A. *Graeco-Roman Funerary Stelae from Upper Egypt.* Liverpool University Press, Liverpool, 1992.

Brown, B. R. *Ptolemaic Painting and Mosaics and the Alexandrian Style.* Cambridge, Massachusetts, 1957. For the Hellenistic stelae and white-ground class cinerary urns.

Hooper, F. A. *Funerary Stelae from Kom Abu-Billou.* Kelsey Museum of Archaeology, Ann Arbor, 1961.

Kamal, A. *Catalogue Général des Antiquités Égyptiennes du Musée du Caire. Stèles Ptolémaiques et Romaines.* Service des Antiquités de l'Égypte, Cairo, 1905. Hieroglyphic stelae.

Sarcophagi, coffins and body cases

Adriani, A. *Repertorio d'Arte dell'Egitto Greco-Romano. Serie A, Volume I–II.* Fondazione (Ignazio Mormino) del Banco di Sicilia, Palermo, 1961. Alexandrian sarcophagi.

Edgar, C. C. *Catalogue Général des Antiquités Égyptiennes du Musée du Caire. Graeco-Egyptian Coffins, Masks and Portraits.* Service des Antiquités de l'Égypte, Cairo, 1905.

Maspero, G. *Catalogue Général des Antiquités Égyptiennes du Musée du Caire. Sarcophages des Époques Persane et Ptolémaique.* Service des Antiquités de l'Égypte, Cairo; volume I, 1913; volume II, 1939.

Masks and portraits

Bierbrier, M. L. (editor). *Portraits and Masks.* British Museum Press, London, 1997.

Doxiadis, E. *The Mysterious Fayum Portraits.* Thames & Hudson, London, 1995.

Grimm, G. *Die römischen Mumienmasken aus Ägypten.* Steiner, Wiesbaden, 1974.

Hawass, Z. *Valley of the Golden Mummies.* Virgin Publishing, London, 2000.

Shore, A. F. *Portrait Painting from Roman Egypt.* The British Museum, 1972.

Walker, S., and Bierbrier, M. *Ancient Faces.* British Museum Press, London, 1997.

Cinerary urns

Cook, B. F. *Inscribed Hadra Vases in the Metropolitan Museum.* The Metropolitan Museum, New York, 1966.

Enklaar, A. 'Chronologie et Peintres des Hydries de Hadra', in *Bulletin Antieke Beschaving,* 60, Leiden, 1985, 106–151.

Enklaar, A. 'Les Hydries de Hadra II: Formes et Ateliers', in *Bulletin Antieke Beschaving,* 61, Leiden, 1986, 41–63.

10
Museums

The largest collections of material from the Graeco-Roman Period in Egypt are held at the three museums in Alexandria, but most museums throughout the world with Egyptian collections have a section displaying finds of the period. The visitor is also advised to visit the sections on Greece and Rome as relevant material from Egypt can often be found there.

United Kingdom

Ashmolean Museum of Art and Archaeology, Beaumont Street, Oxford OX1 2PH. Telephone: 01865 278000. Website: www.ashmol.ox.ac.uk

Birmingham Museum and Art Gallery, Chamberlain Square, Birmingham B3 3DH. Telephone: 0121 303 2834. Website: www.bmag.org.uk

Bolton Museum and Art Gallery, Le Mans Crescent, Bolton, Lancashire BL1 1SE. Telephone: 01204 332211. Website: www.boltonmuseums.org.uk

Bristol's City Museum and Art Gallery, Queen's Road, Bristol BS8 1RL. Telephone: 0117 922 3571. Website: www.bristol-city.gov.uk/museums

The British Museum, Great Russell Street, London WC1B 3DG. Telephone: 020 7323 8000. Website: www.thebritishmuseum.ac.uk

Durham University Oriental Museum, Elvet Hill, Durham DH1 3TH. Telephone: 0191 334 5694. Website: www.dur.ac.uk/orientalmuseum

The Fitzwilliam Museum, Trumpington Street, Cambridge CB2 1RB. Telephone: 01223 332900. Website: www.fitzmuseum.cam.ac.uk

The Manchester Museum, The University of Manchester, Oxford Road, Manchester M13 9PL. Telephone: 0161 275 2634. Website: www.museum.man.ac.uk

Museum of the School of Archaeology, Classics and Egyptology, University of Liverpool, 14 Abercromby Square, Liverpool L69 7WZ. Telephone: 0151 794 2467. Website: www.liv.ac.uk/sace (Appointment necessary. Sculptural stelae from Upper Egypt.)

The Petrie Museum of Egyptian Archaeology, University College London, Malet Place, London WC1E 6BT. Telephone: 020 7679 2884. Website: www.petrie.ucl.ac.uk

Royal Museum of Scotland, Chambers Street, Edinburgh EH1 1JF. Telephone: 0131 247 4422. Website: www.nms.ac.uk

Victoria and Albert Museum, Cromwell Road, South Kensington, London SW7 2RL. Telephone: 020 7942 2000. Website: www.vam.ac.uk

World Museum Liverpool, William Brown Street, Liverpool L3 8EN. Telephone: 0151 478 4393. Website: www.liverpoolmuseums.org.uk

Austria

Kunsthistorisches Museum Wien, Main Building, Maria Theresien-Platz, 1010 Vienna. Website: www.khm.at

Belgium

Musées Royaux d'Art et d'Histoire, Parc du Cinquantenaire 10, 1000 Brussels. Website: www.kmkg-mrah.be

Canada
Royal Ontario Museum, 100 Queen's Park, Toronto, Ontario M5S 2C6. Website: www.rom.on.ca

Egypt
Alexandria National Museum, Fouad Street, Alexandria.
Bahariya Museum, Bawit, Bahariya Oasis. (The Golden Mummies.)
Bibliotheca Alexandrina, PO Box 138, El-Shatby, Alexandria 21256. Website: www.bibalex.org
Coptic Museum, Fakhry Abd el Nour Street No 4, Abbassia, Cairo. Website: www.copticmuseum.gov.eg
The Egyptian National Museum, Midan el-Tahrir, Kasr el-Nil, Cairo 11557. Website: www.egyptianmuseum.gov.cg (Includes original wall paintings from Tuna el-Gebel.)
Graeco-Roman Museum, Mathaf el Romani Street, Downtown, Alexandria. Website: www.grm.gov.eg
Mallawi Antiquities Museum, Corner of Alglaa Street/Elerfany Street, Mallawi, Upper Egypt. (Finds from Tuna el-Gebel.)

France
Musée du Louvre, 75058 Paris Cedex 01. Website: www.louvre.fr

Germany
Ägyptisches Museum, Bodestrasse 1–3, 10178 Berlin. Website: www.smb.spk-berlin.de
Kestner-Museum, Trammplatz 3, 30159 Hannover. Website: www.kestner-museum.de
Roemer und Pelizaeus Museum, Am Steine 1-2, 31134 Hildesheim. Website: www.rpmuseum.de

Greece
Benaki Museum, 1 Koumbari Str and Vas, Sofias Av, 10674 Athens. Website: www.benaki.gr

Republic of Ireland
National Museum of Ireland, Collins Barracks, Benburb Street, Dublin 7. Telephone: (+353) 1 677 7444. Website: www.museum.ie

Italy
Museo Archeologico di Firenze, Via della Colonna 38, 50121 Firenze (Florence). Website: www.firenzemusei.it
Museo Gregoriano Egizio, Musei Vaticani, Rome. Website: www.mv.vatican.va/3
Museo Egizio, Palazzo dell-Accademia delle Scienze, Via Accademia delle Scienze, 10123 Torino (Turin). Website: www.museoegizio.org

Russia
Pushkin State Museum of Fine Arts, Volhonka Strase 12, 119019 Moscow. Website: www.museum.ru/gmii

United States of America

Brooklyn Museum, 200 Eastern Parkway, Brooklyn, New York 11238. Website: www.brooklynmuseum.org

Cleveland Museum of Art, 11150 East Boulevard, Cleveland, Ohio 44106. Website: www.clemusart.com

J. Paul Getty Museum, 1200 Getty Center Drive, Malibu, Los Angeles, California 90094-1687. Website: www.getty.edu

Kelsey Museum of Archaeology, University of Michigan, 434 South State Street, Ann Arbor, Michigan 48109. Website: www.lsa.umich.edu/kelsey (The 'Terenouthis' stelae.)

Metropolitan Museum of Art, 1000 Fifth Avenue at 82nd Street, New York, New York 10028. Website: www.metmuseum.org

Museum of Fine Arts, Avenue of the Arts, 465 Huntington Avenue, Boston, Massachusetts 02115-5597. Website: www.mfa.org

Phoebe Hearst Museum of Anthropology, 102 Kroeber Hall, University of California, Berkeley, California 94720-3712. Website: http://hearstmuseum.berkeley.edu

University of Chicago Oriental Institute Museum, 1155 East 58th Street, Chicago, Illinois 60637. Website: http://oi-uchicago.edu

Acknowledgements

I wish to express my thanks to Miss Patricia Winker of the University of Liverpool, Mrs Angela Thomas and Mr John Rotheroe and his staff at Shire Publications for bringing this work to fruition. I am very grateful to Dr Christina Riggs for reading through the text and providing helpful advice. Special thanks are also due to Derek and Patricia Edwards of Framecraft for photographs, graphic compilations and infinite patience and advice, to Dr John Taylor of the British Museum for providing access and allowing me to photograph exhibits, and to Michael Ackroyd, my friend and facilitator in Egypt. I thank those individuals and institutions who have allowed me to use their illustrations, in particular Mrs Angela Thomas (Bolton Museum), Dr Christina Riggs (Manchester Museum), Robert Partridge (Ancient Egypt Picture Library), Margaret Wilson and Helen Nicoll (National Museums of Scotland), and Dr Peter Dixon. For on-site access and assistance, I thank Dr Steven Snape (University of Liverpool, Zawiyet umm el-Rakham), Osama Sallam (Egyptian Antiquities Service, Mersa Matruh), Colin Clement (Centre d'Études Alexandrines), Rafal Czerner (Polish Mission's excavations at Marina el-Alamein), and Dr Ahmed Abd el-Fattah (Graeco-Roman Museum, Alexandria) for his advice on extant Alexandrian tombs. I also thank Professor Christopher Mee of the University of Liverpool, who supervised my MPhil thesis, and Dr Penelope Wilson (Durham University) and the late Dr Dominic Montserrat for their advice and encouragement. The chronology is based on that of Dr William J. Murnane and Simon P. Ellis and acknowledgement is made to them and Penguin Books for its use here.

Index

Page numbers in italic refer to illustrations.